The Marriage-Friendly Church

a distinct voice for marriage in the 21st century church

DANIEL F. CAMP

Unless otherwise specified, the people, events, and churches mentioned as examples in this book are fictitious and only serve to illustrate a point. Any similarities are coincidental.

ISBN: 978-0-89098-535-9

2809 12th Ave S, Nashville, TN 37204

Cover design by Jonathan Edelhuber

Dedication

To my beautiful, wonderful wife—I would not fully understand God's love, forgiveness, grace, mercy, goodness, and kindness apart from my relationship with Lisa. I love you.

My wonderful children, Chloe, Macie, and Holden, who have helped me to better understand God as my Father, and who have brought me unbelievable joy. I pray constantly that, if it is my children's calling, God is even now preparing two young men and one young lady to be their future mates.

Acknowledgements

Thanks to everyone who helped make this book a reality. Though she would never take credit, my wife Lisa's hand is all throughout this work. I am forever indebted to my parents Jim and Edith Camp who raised me to know and love the Lord, and who lived marriage as a Kingdom calling even if they never would have labeled it as such.

I humbly thank the past and present ministers and elders at the Smyrna church of Christ, who have a passion for the Kingdom of God and have encouraged my work in marriage ministry. It is a blessing to serve with them all. Also, I am so very, very appreciative of the wonderful brothers and sisters at Smyrna who have constantly encouraged me, have patiently sat through classes, retreats, and workshops, and have helped me shape my theology of marriage.

To the faculty and staff of the Graduate School of Theology at ACU (especially the late Charles Siburt), thank you for pushing me on when I was ready to settle for too little. My D. Min cohort—Jason, Nathan, David, Drew, Charlton, and Bob—thanks for listening to me "wax eloquently" about marriage ministry during our years at ACU and thanks for your feedback along the way writing this book.

I owe a debt of gratitude to Marc Jones and John Temple. After twenty-plus years of weekly lunches together, I can't tell you how much your friendship and feedback means to me. To John Grant and Gary Hickerson, thanks for being sounding boards and mentors.

And finally, thanks to 21st Century Christian for being a blessing to me. Tom's faith in me, encouragement, and patience with me have kept me excited and motivated. May God bless our efforts to strengthen marriages in His Kingdom.

Table of Contents

Foreword

One day I was visiting my local Christian bookstore. I stood looking at a large shelf of books labeled "Church." Sections were tagged with subcategories of "church growth," and "missional church," and many more similarly appealing designations. Those books told me everything from how to welcome visitors and make them want to come back to how to take the gospel to the neighborhood next door to the church building. For church leaders, there was a wealth of good information on what it means to be a godly, vibrant, active, church community.

Directly across the aisle from the "Church" section was the "Love, Marriage, and Relationships" section. Books abounded on getting ready for marriage, the joys of marriage, handling conflict, couples finding time for themselves, and even dealing with in-laws. There were also books on separation, divorce, remarriage, and other painful elements of marriage in a fallen world. These books also contained a wealth of information directed at couples to bring counsel, advice, and hope.

But for all the good advice to leaders found in the "church" section, and all the good advice found for individual couples in the "marriage" section, there was nothing to bridge the two sections. We need books for church leaders about what it means to be the church God is calling us to be. We need books for couples that talk about marriage the way God intends for it to be. But we also need something that brings the two together and looks at marriage from a church perspective; something that demands churches take the lead in making marriage a part of the overall church context; something that demands that churches take responsibility in becoming proactive in building healthier, kingdom-centered marriages; something that says marriage is the church's business, and the church will honor God by tending to marriage.

Lord willing, this book will bridge that gap between church and marriage and lead us forward.

Introduction and Purpose

Let me start out by explaining what this book is not. This book is not a couples' guide to a better marriage. It is not a quick fix program. It is not a nice, clean, easy, programmatic step-by-step, hassle-free plan for designing and implementing a church-wide marriage ministry. You will not find "30 Days to a Great Marriage Ministry" in the pages that follow. This book is also not a cookie cutter system. It would be foolish to think marriage ministry at a congregation of twenty-five will look like marriage ministry at a congregation of two thousand. Nor will a marriage ministry in rural Tennessee mirror a marriage ministry in New York City or Los Angeles. What you will find in this book is not something that you will achieve easily or solely by your own efforts. If you try to separate this (or any) ministry from God's Word, God's power, and God's Spirit, you will find that what you achieve is not what you are hoping for. This book is also not something you can read once, apply once, or think about once and expect to make any kind of a lasting difference.

So what is this book then? This book is an invitation. It is an invitation for the leadership and membership of every church into the wonderful world of marriage ministry. We believe God created marriage, don't we? We believe God has a plan and purpose for marriage, don't we? We believe God hates divorce and wants marriages to last "till death do we part," don't we? Of course we do. But what are we willing to do about it? That is the invitation of this book; to do something about it! To become proactive in encouraging, strengthening, and enhancing marriage as a God-created, God-given covenant relationship. To become purposeful in helping couples recognize their place in growing the kingdom of God through strong, healthy, and joyful Christian marriages. To reclaim marriage. Reclaim it as a vibrant part of who you are as the body of Christ.

What you will find in these pages is for ministers, elders, deacons, church leaders, those who have been married for less than a year, and those who have been married for over fifty years. It is for those who have walked the line of divorce but found reconciliation, and for those who know firsthand the pain of divorce. It is for those who have made mistakes in their own marriage relationships that they do not want anyone else to ever repeat. It is for those with solid marriages and for those who are struggling and are looking to their spiritual family for hope. It is for rural country churches with less than twenty-five members, for large urban churches with thousands of members, and for every congregation size in between. In short, it is for anyone with a passion for God-centered, life-changing marriage ministry. It is a guide to a careful analysis of what your church is really saying about marriage, and whether or not you have bought the world's way of experiencing marriage or if you are seeking something better. It is a guide to being proactive and purposeful in how the church encounters marriage in a culture that far more frequently embraces matrimony as a social arrangement rather than a spiritual calling.

There is a tag line that Remembering Our First Love Marriage Ministries likes to use: *Strong marriages equal strong families. Strong families equal strong churches. Strong churches equal strong communities.* It begins with strong marriages. This in no way minimizes those who are called to remain single, but singles ministry is someone else's book. So, please prayerfully and purposefully join us on the journey to restore a distinct voice of marriage to the church that belongs to the One who created marriage.

Chapter 1

Why Do We Need This?
Recognizing the Two Battlefronts

The Cultural Battlefront and the Line We've Been Fed

"Man-made prisons" is the way Cosmo Kramer described marriage to Jerry in a classic episode of *Seinfeld*. Audrey is okay with her husband Jeff going to strip clubs as long as he observes the "look but don't touch" rule on *Rules of Engagement*. On *Glee*, Kendra tells her sister Terri (who is faking a pregnancy to try and keep husband Will interested in her) that "lies and deceit are food for marriage; without it a marriage will die." How many more examples can easily be pulled from any night of television, whether network TV, basic cable, or premium pay channels?

Just think about the portrayal of marriage on television over the years. The stable marriages and nuclear families of the 1950s and 60s sitcoms seem to be a thing of the past. But even those shows usually portrayed a dominating husband who ruled over a wife who basically had no say in their relationship. Jump ahead a few decades, and things have changed. In shows where you can find a nuclear family, dad is often shown as a buffoon, spouses lie to each other, and the view of marriage is manipulative and self-serving with little or no respect for the other partner. Yes, I realize it is all done in the name of comedy or drama or art, but at what expense? What is the message our kids are receiving about marriage? Is this distorted message about marriage silently and steadily creeping into our own relationships even as we pipeline it into our homes through our televisions?

What does television serve up when it comes to intimacy in marriage? In 2008, the Parent's Television Counsel issued a comprehensive report concerning sexual content on the major networks (parentstv.org/ptc/publications/reports/sexontv/marriagestudy.pdf). Eagleforum.org's website reported on the findings and said:

> To hear the major networks tell it, sex within marriage is either a burden or nonexistent, while adultery and extramarital sex are exciting and positive experiences for the people involved. Across hundreds of hours of programming, references to nonmarital sex outnumbered references to marital sex by three to one—and by almost four to one during the "family hour" between 8:00 and 9:00 p.m, EST. There were twice as many references to adultery as to married sex. When references to marital sex did crop up, they were usually negative (www.eagleforum.org/educate/2008/oct08/TV-shows.html).

What about music? Like most television depictions of marriage, mainstream music praises selfish relationships that are destructive to godly marriage, relegating relationships to nothing more than sexual encounters. Along with their lust-charged lyrics, the personalities behind the music tout a similar abhorrence toward marriage. Gene Simmons, the lead singer for the rock band KISS, who has publically stated that men should not be expected to be monogamous, said,

"Marriage is a wonderful institution, but I've heard you've gotta be nuts to be in an institution." From iconic rockers of the past to today's latest flavor of the month, the personalities behind the music often embody the anti-marriage lyrics they belt out. But this is what our kids are listening to. This is what we are listening to.

The silver screen is ripe with movies that set committed marriage aside for self-serving sexual encounters. Hollywood adores a good love story, but shallow romanticism is the norm and positive portrayals of marriage are the rare exception. "Friends with benefits" and "no strings attached" are not just catchphrases; they are multimillion dollar investments by studios into the appeal of sexual relationships devoid of the commitment of marriage.

Perhaps most destructive to marriage has been the explosive growth of the internet. It is difficult to put definitive numbers on how many pornographic websites there are. First, statistics are notoriously easy to manipulate. Some reports say only about 10% of websites are pornographic. Other reports say as much as 50% are adult oriented. It is difficult to try to calculate percentages based on simple keyword searches, as context often determines what a site is advocating. A search for "breasts" might reveal a staggering number of adult-oriented sites, but it might also reveal web pages with information for breast cancer survivors. Should Ebay be considered a pornographic site because they allow the sale of *Playboy*, or because they have an "adult verification" portion to their website?

A second difficulty arises in defining what constitutes pornography? While most of us have a clear idea of our own definition of pornography, there is little consensus from person to person. For example, Leonardo da Vinci's *Vitruvian Man*—you know the man inside the square inside of a circle—is universally recognized as a great work of art. Yet it shows a full frontal view of male genitalia. Should websites that show pictures of Michelangelo's *David* sculpture, or Adam's nakedness depicted on the ceiling of the Sistine Chapel, or

Edouard Manet's *Le déjeuner sur l'herbe,* or a host of other classic artworks be considered pornographic? Does it become pornography when the images are of live models rather than depictions in some other artistic medium? Does the intention have to be for illicit sexual gratification for something to be considered pornographic, or does any depiction of nudity qualify? And how much flesh being exposed is too much? Where does soft core pornography begin? Do sites with lingerie ads count as adult websites? Is pornography just visual images, or does it also include the written word that is meant to excite and titillate?

Regardless of the exact statistics or the exact definition of pornography, there is no doubt that the internet provides a plethora of opportunities for accessing it. Pornographic addiction is growing, and not just among men. Women are becoming increasingly hooked. The damaging effects of pornography on marriage are amplified by both the ease of access and the relative secrecy provided by the internet. Gone are the days of a teenage boy hiding a magazine under his mattress. Children are computer savvy enough to quickly learn how to both find and cover up anything they want to see, so pornography's poisonous roots can begin early and run deep and strong. Exposure creates acceptance, and many consider pornography no big deal—perhaps even a colloquially celebrated rite of passage—especially in the years leading up to marriage.

So, does life imitate the media, or does the media imitate life? I don't know. What I do know is that our churches are full of people who have bought into the media's version of relationships, marriage, love, and intimacy, and it is leaving broken homes, damaged children, and painful divorces in its wake. Whether it is television, music, movies, or the internet, the strongest voices in our culture are working far more actively *against* healthy marriages than working *for* strong marriages. Sadly, I know by the time this book sees print, my media references and statistics will be outdated. Even sadder, I expect you can fill in the television, movies, music, and technology culture of your own time and it will probably be even more detrimental to Christian marriage relationships.

But this battlefield is not limited to the media. Other cultural voices constantly shout conflicting messages about marriage. Homosexuality, co-habitation, materialism, individualism, racism, social status, regional norms and taboos, family pressures, and a multitude of other voices form a cacophony of influences that shape how we view and experience marriage. The contemporary western culture will always be a battlefield against healthy marriage.

The Forgotten Battlefield

Red Alert! Red Alert! The Reactive Nature of Churches

In Matthew 16, Jesus asks his disciples a simple question. "Who do people say I am?" After they share a short list of past and contemporary prophets, Jesus asks a follow up question. "Who do you say I am?" When Peter acknowledges that Jesus is the Christ of God, the foundation of the gospel message, Jesus goes on to establish the church on that gospel claim. But Jesus doesn't want his church to be a cowardly lot, afraid of the culture, afraid of the world. He wants his church to be salt and light in the world in such a powerful way that Hades itself will recoil in fear.

You see, gates are a defensive barrier, and Jesus clearly said even those protective gates of Hades will not be able to stop the powerfully spreading gospel. The message of Christ and the redemption he brings, the alternative to the world's empty way of life, will powerfully shatter any stronghold that tries to stand against it.

But somewhere between the time Jesus said those words and today, we have changed the meaning. In fact, many have taken this passage to mean the exact opposite. Rather than a forcefully advancing message of hope and healing, we have interpreted the Scripture to mean the forces of Hades are constantly pounding at our door, shoving their gates ever outward. But fear not, so long as we huddle together in our concrete bunkers, tell each other everything is okay, and loudly sing our hymns to pacify each other, then Hades won't get in here. In so many ways, we went from a *proactive* gospel message ("Rejoice, the gates of Hades cannot stand up against us!") to a *reactive* church culture ("Oh no, the gates of Hades are crushing in on us!"). And this reactive mode affects the way the church views Christian marriage. Let's face it. Most churches are reactive when it comes to marriage. Consider the case of Julianne and David.

Julianne and David were the storybook couple. They met their freshman year at a Christian college and became instant friends. A solid friendship for two years nurtured feelings that led to a year of dating, followed by a nine-month engagement, and finally a wedding two weeks after graduation.

Fast forward fourteen years, David and Julianne have a twelve-year-old son and an eight- year-old daughter, with a third child on the way. David is a deacon in their local church, which they have been an active part of since moving into the community ten years ago. He is involved with the youth ministry, chaperoning youth events and acting as a powerful, positive role model for the teens. As a stay-at-home mom, Julianne appears to be the perfect mother, always doting on her children. She volunteers with several ministries each week, and is a constant, welcomed presence around the church building. Both David and Julianne teach Bible classes regularly. In short, they are the kind of couple that every church would like to have in abundance.

At least that is what everyone believed—including their closest friends—until the night Julianne called her best friend, sobbing uncontrollably. After calming Julianne down, her friend listened in shock as Julianne said David had packed his bags and left her for another woman that he had been sexually involved with for the past three months. She confessed that their marriage had been in absolute shambles for the past eighteen months and many of the root causes of their problems could be traced back nearly a decade.

Sadly, by changing just a few details, nearly every church can identify at least one, if not multiple couples, who echo David and Julianne's story. Not every situation involves adultery. Not every couple has children. Not every couple is as visibly involved in church activities as David and Julianne. But the story is still the same.

We look at the couples in our church and assume that everything is good. But why wouldn't we? Everyone else is playing the same game that we are. We have created a shame culture that expects everyone to put on their "church face." We go to church, put on our church faces, talk our church talk, and act the way we are expected to act. So, no one is any the wiser about the fight we had on the way to church this morning, the financial difficulties that are threatening to take our home, the far-too-flirtatious co-worker that beckons to us every day, or the excessive discipline problem we've been experiencing with our teenage daughter. We smile, enthusiastically say "Fine!" when asked "How are you?" and then go back to marriages that are drained, strained, and often in pain. The church, which should be an oasis of help and hope and healing, instead becomes a part of the problem. The shame of not being perfect stares us in the face, as everyone else pretends to be perfect to avoid that same shame.

Then, when a couple that has been married twenty years parts ways, we shake our heads in disbelief. *"They seemed so happy. Who would have seen that coming?"* When two or three couples' relationships all explode within a reasonably short amount of time, we become alarmed. *"How could this be happening at our church?"* When five couples are in deep marital distress, we react! *"Why hasn't something been done sooner? We need a series of sermons on Christian marriage."* We want bulletin articles, classes, or to bring in guest speakers who are experts in marriage. We are reactive. And for those couples in distress, by the time we decide to do something, it is often too late. The gates of hades have come to us.

Not all couples are putting on a church face; some really are doing well. Not all couples are hurting. But on the other side of the coin, not all long-term marriages are healthy. Not all couples that will never divorce are happily married. With the state of marriage being such a mixed bag, what is the church to do? As much as it might pain us to admit it, the forgotten battlefield that is crippling Christian marriages is often our own churches. But how? How can we be damaging to that which we know we love and hold so dear? How can church be bad for marriage? Whether we want to admit it or not, our church culture typically mimics society's distorted views of marriage. While it is common in Bible classes and sermons to criticize the secular culture for championing sexual promiscuity and deviance, and compromising and belittling the marriage covenant relationship, the secular culture has still permeated the church. The entertainment industry, the pornography industry, and the media have a profound effect on marital views and practices within a congregation. Acceptable norms within the church are often defined by outside sources as often as they are by Scripture. These changing norms include views on the permanency of marriage and views on appropriate conduct for premarital relationships, homosexuality, what constitutes infidelity, and challenges from technology, among others.

When we see the church's view and practice of marriage being redefined, the natural response for a reactive church culture is to take a defensive stance. We don't want to lose any more ground, so we plan classes and sermons on marriage. We want our members to understand that relationships take work. But we become so adamant in that pursuit that we unintentionally paint marriage in a negative light. To be honest, I am tired of lesson after lesson that delves into the struggles, hardships, and sacrifices of marriage. Mind you, I'm not blind to the realities of marriage and the challenges a relationship presents, but when our church culture continually casts this God-given covenant union in a negative light, then how do we expect our members to ever see marriage as anything other than a burden. You are not alone if you have ever left a sermon on marriage thinking, "Wow, this relationship is a real trial. Thank God one of us will eventually be dead and the other will finally be free!" I'd love to hear more lessons that portray "Till death do we part" as a blessed promise rather than a dreaded sentence.

Certainly, our church culture does not intentionally set out to harm marriages. But what hinders the church's viability in fostering godly, Christian marriage? Along with the church's reactive stance toward marriage, the perpetuation of the "church face" shame culture that it creates within our churches, the secular culture's growing influence on the church, and negatively-based teaching about marriage, several other key factors appear far too often.

A church can perpetuate divisive ministry structures that are harmful to marriage. In many churches, couples are confused about how to be involved in the congregation in healthy ways. Typically, when a couple joins a congregation, husband and wife are introduced to an organized pathway into congregational involvement. New families sit down with someone who provides them with a list of ministries the congregation offers and asks the couple where they would like to become active. Often, there is a men's track and a women's track for involvement, and these tracks are frequently very different in what is and is not offered. Thus the men's sheet is filled with ways to be involved in the public worship assembly, building maintenance, handyman-type activities, and various other things typically reserved for men. The women's involvement encompasses preparing food for the infirmed or bereaved, sending cards, sewing, or other domestic skills. The two ministry paths might cross over in a limited number of arenas such as chaperoning youth events or possibly teaching a class, but the language of the new members' orientation and involvement usually does not convey couple's ministry. Areas of couple's ministry are the exception rather than the norm, and depending on the traditions of a given fellowship or congregation a man or woman's role might be further limited.

A congregation's full church calendar can also be harmful to strong marriages. Members tend to measure a person's worth and commitment by how busy he or she is. It is in this misguided belief that the (oftentimes) marriage-devouring separate ministry tracks mentioned above feed and thrive. When an overloaded church calendar is coupled with a family calendar that is filled with sports events, school events, work events, and social events, husbands and wives can find themselves constantly running in different directions.

The real bane of the church calendar is the false impression that participation in church activities is the same as participation in the kingdom of God, and to skip a church event is equal to rebellion against what God desires for one's marriage and family. Ironically, most church calendars are so age segregated for children and gender segregated for adults that the feeling is unjustified, as church activities often cause division in marriages and families rather than unity. The church calendar can easily create a stigma of guilt for "not being committed to God" even as it unknowingly harms a marriage and/or family. This is an area that is personally difficult for me. Because our society believes that busyness equals worth, there is a sense from many church leaders that if we do not produce a fully loaded calendar, the congregation will question our worth to the church as paid staff, or, if a volunteer, our dedication in leading a ministry. It is difficult to lead people into seeing, let alone experiencing, a better way when that way is so counter-cultural. It is easier for most church leaders to perpetuate the marriage-killing busyness than it is to take on the challenge of leading the congregation into a means to deeper, better relationships.

Even with all of the above at play, the most detrimental blow to the vast majority of churches is a missing or floundering theology of marriage. Because we value marriage and understand the spiritual significance of healthy marriages to a healthy congregation, most churches believe they do have a theology of marriage. However, how well-defined, well-articulated, and well-implemented is it? Some churches do have a theology of divorce and remarriage; a guiding belief about what are and are not acceptable reasons for a marriage to end, and what that means to a divorced individual's participation in the community life of the congregation. But a theology of divorce and remarriage is not the same as a theology of marriage. A theology of divorce and remarriage is reactive, outlining a church's response to a marriage that is already broken. A theology of marriage is proactive. Because this is such a critical area, chapter six will more fully address marriage theology.

Is something amiss in our churches? Do we need to do something different? Does the church need to *be* something different? Is there a church culture regarding marriage (that we all know exists, yet rarely talk about) that needs to be examined, put on trial, and perhaps even convicted and eradicated?

Almost half the marriages in America end in divorce. This statistic is actually down from previous years, but the decline is not a reason to rejoice. The decline in divorces is due to an increase in unmarried couples living together. This attitude of foregoing marriage and living together is not foreign to people professing to be Christians. Even among people raised in the Christian faith, an ever-increasing number are embracing living together outside of marriage, engaging in sexual activity, and enjoying all the benefits of marriage apart from the covenant commitment. "For better or for worse," has become "As long as it is convenient and satisfies me."

According to a 1999 poll of 3,854 people conducted by George Barna, the divorce rate among born again Christians was actually higher than the divorce rate experienced by the rest of the country. In commenting on his findings, Barna said,

> While it may be alarming to discover that born again Christians are more likely than others to experience a divorce, that pattern has been in place for quite some time...the research also raises questions regarding the effectiveness of how churches minister to families. The ultimate responsibility for a marriage belongs to the husband and wife, ***but the high incidence of divorce within the Christian community challenges the idea that churches provide truly practical and life-changing support for marriages.*** (Emphasis mine)

In April of 2008 in a similar poll of 5,017 people, Barna found an even more disturbing trend developing:

> Interviews with young adults suggest that they want their initial marriage to last, but are not particularly optimistic about that possibility...There is also evidence that many young people are moving toward embracing the idea of serial marriage, in which a person gets married two or three times, seeking a different partner for each phase of their adult life.

Not only have many young Christians accepted divorce as inevitable, some are even planning for it!

If you think this is not your church or your community, then I would challenge you to try this little experiment. Contact the churches in your community. Ask them two simple questions: 1) On a scale of 1 to 10, how important are healthy marriages to your congregation's well being? and, 2) What are you doing as a congregation to insure healthy marriages? A few years ago, when I asked those questions to twenty-three churches from my fellowship in my immediate area, this is what I found. Of those twenty-three churches, all of them said that strong marriages were absolutely vital to the health of the congregation. However, out of those same twenty-three congregations, only two (my own congregation being one of them) were doing anything to strengthen and encourage healthy marriages in a purposeful manner. Do you see the problem? Twenty-three adamantly said healthy marriages were essential to a healthy congregation. One preaching minister even said that it comes up at almost every leadership meeting he attends. But only two (and this brother's church was *not* one of the two) are doing anything about it in a deliberate, purposeful, proactive manner. On the whole, churches are reactive.

This is not to say that there are not marriage classes, sermons, retreats, seminars, and other good things going on among churches. And I have no doubts that those events are working to develop strong marriages in the kingdom of God. But what about the church itself? Are those events reactive or proactive? Is there anything fundamentally different from the world's experience of marriage in the way your church teaches about marriage, equips couples for marriage, and provides the means for couples to have Christ-centered marriages that help grow the kingdom of God? Is a healthy theology and practice of marriage a part of the fabric of who you are as a congregation? Virtually every church has at least some basic building blocks on which to begin forming a powerful marriage ministry, but proactive, purposeful marriage ministry is the exception, not the norm.

What you can and cannot do

If you want to see your church engage in a powerful marriage ministry, you must first recognize that there are several things which you can and cannot do. The first thing you cannot do, is you cannot make a couple do anything they do not want to do to save or strengthen their marriage. As much as we would like to change others, we can only change ourselves. Second, you cannot change anyone's background. The experiences your individual members bring to the table will always affect those people's individual marriages and the entire congregation's marriage ministry. Each person is a product of what has happened to him or her, and your church's community life is a sum of those individual parts. However, that doesn't mean you are doomed to follow a specific path. Third, you cannot prevent marital problems or divorces from occurring within your church. Sin and selfishness are a part of living in a fallen world, and regrettably, those terrible traits of our "Adam-and-Eve-ness" manifest themselves in marriage, and sometimes far more frequently in marriage than in any other relationship.

If I cannot make couples do anything they do not want to do, and I cannot prevent divorces and marital strife, what's the point of this book? Well, there definitely are things you can do. A reactive church focuses on what they *cannot* do. A proactive church focuses on what they *can* do. First, you can create a climate in which marriage is honored at your church. Second, you can help change decades of bad church culture by promoting openness and honesty in dealing with marital issues. Third, you can lead by example, being honest about the state of your own marriage and determining you are going to make your marriage all it can be. Fourth, you can provide the tools and resources to help couples have a God-centered marriage. You can help couples see marriage as more than a contract, but instead a joyful, blessed, life-long covenant relationship meant to bring glory to God. You can advance marriage as a unique calling for a husband and wife's joint participation in the kingdom of God.

Ask yourself the following questions. Is my congregation fundamentally different from the world in the way we view marriage, honor marriage, and treat the marriage covenant? How would it change the way I minister if I'm not always stomping out marriage fires? How would it change our youth ministry if the kids had more stable homes? How would it change the focus of all of our ministries, the number of volunteers, and the spirit of serving for the kingdom of God if we had less marital conflict? Is the marriage ministry at your congregation proactive or reactive?

If the best defense is a good offense, it is time to defend marriage by taking the offense in teaching about, encouraging, and growing healthy, godly marriages. In the following chapters, I will outline an assessment process that, if followed, will move your congregation from reactive defensiveness to a proactive momentum. As I said before, this process will take time and effort, but the transformation it can bring to your congregation will be well worth the sacrifice.

Chapter 2

Changing the Church Marriage Culture

Getting the Cart before the Horse

In 1990, my friend Darren and I went from Nashville, Tennessee to Biloxi, Mississippi for spring break. On the last day of spring break, Darren and I started on the eight hour drive home. Before we left, we failed to ask directions or consult a map, as we thought we knew which way to go (remember, this was before the days of GPS, MapQuest, and everyone having cell phones). After an hour or so of aimless driving, we were hopelessly lost. Being intelligent college students, we knew that Tennessee was north of Mississippi, and Nashville was east of Biloxi. So, we started following every road sign that said "north" or "east," blazing our way down some of the most secluded, rural highways we had ever seen. After several hours of driving, we eventually came to a gas station and asked the attendant what was the quickest way to the interstate. He directed us to I-65. Had we followed our current plan of following highway signs that said "north" or "east," we would have eventually found our way home, but it certainly would have been the long way around. Once we hit I-65 and saw recognizable town names and consistent mileage markers, we had a good reasonable idea about where we actually were. From that, we did a much better job of focusing on where we wanted to go and how long it would take us to actually get there.

The leadership of a church can cast a powerful vision of where they want to be in their marriage ministry, but if they have never made an honest assessment of where they currently are, the route to that destination is infinitely more difficult. Because we value marriage, because we believe marriage to be a good gift from God, and because our default is to be reactive, we want to rush to get something done. There is a temptation to skip the preliminary work and go straight to programming; but you will be better served by laying a strong foundation so that the marriage ministry you build will stand. As hard as it is to do, especially if you see strained marriages all around you, you must first honestly assess where you are now so that you can map out where you must next go.

The first three phases of this process that are outlined in the next few chapters are the foundational work every church needs to go through. It is hard work that will take time and honest assessment. Whether you are just starting a marriage ministry or whether you feel your congregation already has a successful ministry going, paying attention and working through this process will give you clear understanding of where you really are so that you can establish a more intentional plan to get to where you want to go.

Beginning the Process

The moment you begin the process, good people with good intentions will begin to question why your church needs to invest time and energy into creating (or improving) a proactive marriage ministry. The following are all things you might hear if marriage ministry begins to move toward a more prominent, proactive position in the life of the congregation:

- Everything is fine. Why do we need to be investing time in this when there are lost souls out there?
- We don't have those marriage problems here.
- We're too old to change our ways. Besides, why mess with things now? We've learned to be content with it the way it is.
- If you keep telling people they can be happier in their marriage, you'll only make them miserable trying to measure up to someone with a better marriage.
- I don't want to hear a sermon about marriage every week! (and the preacher might be tempted to say "I don't want to preach a sermon about marriage every week!")

You will likely hear all of these things as well as dozens of other comments. While you will want to prepare yourself to answer any potential questions, remember, the people who seemed to be undermining your efforts are not against strong, healthy, godly marriages. More than likely, their experience has been the typical reactive church stance of "everything's fine," and they do not know any other way. After all, it is always easier to be reactive than proactive.

Making the commitment

If you are tired of not being able to tell the difference between a Christian couple and any other couple, if you are tired of settling for relationships that are far less than what God intends for marriage, if you are tired of a church that is reactive rather than proactive, then do something about it. But understand this; just like marriage itself, a proactive marriage ministry is a lifetime commitment. That of course doesn't mean that you will necessarily have to be in a leadership position with the marriage ministry forever, but it does mean that you are committing to becoming a part of a positive force for marriage at your church, whether you are leading or not. You are signing on to be proactive, purposeful, and exemplify the godly, strong, healthy marriages that will become a significant part of the fabric of who you are as a church.

It is vital at the outset that the leadership of your church is willing to be a part of this commitment. If healthy marriages are not a priority to your church leadership, then you will find yourself facing an uphill battle. That is not to say that every elder or deacon or church leader will immediately embrace the path to proactive marriage ministry (you may have to get them to that point through the process described in the following chapters), but they must at least initially acknowledge the need for a proactive marriage ministry as a means of the church reclaiming a distinct voice in our culture.

As you begin to contemplate your commitment to this process, it will be beneficial to write it down. This way, you can keep it in front of you as a reminder of why you are reading this book, investing this time and energy, trying to persuade people of the need for a proactive marriage ministry, and giving of yourself to change your church forever. A written commitment doesn't have to be long or complicated. It does not have to spell out every single aspect of your journey in this ministry. It just needs to be something concrete and tangible enough to keep you on the right track; something that helps you keep a clear focus. Such a written commitment might be something as simple as this:

> This is not a "quick fix" one time program or event meant to take care of all this church's marriage problems. Rather it is an invitation to an ongoing ministry that should be foundational to this church's identity. Both success and failure will flow from this ministry, but the driving force that will keep us going is a heart for and commitment to God's purpose and design for marriage.

Obviously, you will need to find your own motivation for this commitment, but whatever it is, keep it in front of you constantly.

Forming the team

Unless your congregation is made up of your own family and no one else, you are going to want to assemble a team. Your team needs to have some church leaders and their spouses. You need couples who have been married a long time and couples who might still qualify as newlyweds. You want couples with solid marriages, but also couples who have been through storms that have threatened to destroy their marriages. You will want couples who are committed to healthy marriages. You will want couples who are not content with the status quo. You will want couples who come from a variety of backgrounds that are willing to minister and, if needed, be ministered to themselves. Above all else, you need couples who love the Lord and believe that God created marriage to be something powerfully wonderful for both husband and wife.

The variety of backgrounds, ages, and experiences is necessary for a strong marriage ministry. If all the couples on your team have been married for less than ten years and are DINKS (**D**ual **I**ncome **N**o **K**id**S**), they may be able to steer your church toward great conversations about exciting romantic love, but they may not yet fully understand the sacrificial nature of a long-term marriage relationship. If your team is only composed of older couples, you could have powerful discussions on what it really means to love someone for the long haul, but you may miss out on cultural nuances affecting marriage with which younger generations are so familiar. If your team is only made up of couples who have never gone through any real storms in their marriage, you might have solid examples of marriage to put before the church, but you might also lack any real examples of reconciliation, forgiveness, and healing that is desperately needed in so many other marriages.

It is vitally important that you have couples, not just from various age ranges, but also from differing backgrounds. We tend to want to project our view of marriage on others. So, if every couple on your team grew up in a middle class home with Ward and June Cleaver or Cliff and Clair Huxtable for parents, it is very unlikely you will be able to fully meet the marriage dynamics of your congregation. Without diversity, the things that bring your marriage ministry to life might unintentionally be tailored only toward those who are middle class or above, leaving the impression (as a brother of mine sarcastically said), "I guess this marriage stuff is just for the rich folks." Everything from socio-economic status to ethnic diversity should be considered when forming your team. If your team is not a microcosm of your entire congregation, you will not have a complete picture of marriages within your church from which to begin.

Most significantly, your team should be willing to minister, but they must also be willing to be ministered to. Just as Jethro soundly advised Moses to let others help him (Exodus 18), your team must be willing to receive the grace of being ministered to as much as they are willing to impart the grace of ministering to others. Otherwise you will quickly find yourself with a team that is burnt out and unable to help move the marriage ministry forward in a meaningful way.

As noted above, the most important aspect of each and every person on your team must be their commitment to the Lord, and their firm belief that God, through Christ, has created marriage to be something infinitely better than what the world presents marriage to be. If we are content with marriages that are less than all they can and should be, then we are resigned to reactive defeat. Please don't misinterpret what I mean here. I am not saying marriage has to be perfect for it to be joyful, wonderful, or for a couple to be powerfully engaged in the kingdom of God. But to know that a marriage relationship can and should be better, and then to resign one's self to letting it be less than it can be is to deny the transformative power of Christ to change human relationships for the better.

On a final note regarding your team, start out with the understanding that the team needs to bring in new couples periodically. Too many times in churches, ministries become defined by a person or group of people rather than the purpose of the ministry. This is not to say the marriage ministry will not need strong leadership, but good leaders will understand that young couples do not always remain young couples. Older couples cannot always mentor and provide guidance in the same capacity. And for all couples, life happens. So, if the ministry is dependent on the person rather than the purpose, the distractions of life can derail all the good intentions. What could have been a continuing, powerful, proactive marriage ministry, will die if new couples are not periodically brought in and others groomed for leadership.

As you go through the process outlined ahead and assess your congregation, *The Marriage Ministry Team Workbook* is a valuable resource. This workbook will help your team to remain organized and focused, keeping everyone on track and united. The workbook puts all of the major elements of the assessment outlined in this book at your fingertips in a compact, concise, and easily accessible format, reminding the members of your marriage ministry team of both the "why are we doing this" and "how do we do this" aspects of the process.

Chapter 3

Phase 1: The Whispers in the Hallways

The toughest part of deciding who to vote for is discerning whether or not you really believe what the candidate is saying. It would be difficult to count the number of times we hear about broken promises, reversal of a key position that got someone elected, or a politician talking out both sides of his or her mouth. Have you ever wondered if your church is doing the same thing in regard to marriage? I don't think any church means to do it, but sometimes the message we think we are presenting about marriage may not be what a visitor in our midst would actually hear.

So how do we know what we're actually saying? By listening. This beginning part of the assessment process is the listening phase. And the first thing you will want to listen to is the informal voices of marriage in your congregation. It is what I call "the whispers in the hallways." The informal voices of marriage, or "whispers in the hallway," are the ways the people in your congregation talk about and treat marriage. They are the things they say seriously and in jest. It is the attitude they project about marriage. It is what is casually remarked rather than formally declared. It is what is said before and after worship and what is said informally in a Bible class setting. It is how church members talk about marriage during informal times at the church building and how they talk about marriage at the ball field. It is the "spirit" of marriage at your church, revealing the attitudes members convey about their experience and perception of the marriage covenant; what it means to them personally, and what (if any) affect the congregation has on their experience and perception.

The objective in this first phase is not to build a case for any particular predominant mindset about marriage being in the congregation, but just to listen. You are not seeking to influence anything at this point, and as hard as it is to resist the impulse, you must also remember at this stage you are NOT looking for fixes, just taking in information.

It is critical in this phase to listen to as many voices as possible—old, young, married, divorced, single; all of them say something about the perception of marriage at your church. Remember, this phase is not a witch hunt fueled by a watchdog attitude, but it is being sensitive to the actual state of marriage that is present in your congregation. Sometimes that reality will be a pleasant voice. Other times it will be a harsh voice you might not want to hear. Whatever you discover, it is necessary for you to hear it. You cannot map out your journey to your destination until you accurately pinpoint your actual location.

A word about gathering information

The first phase should last anywhere from eight to twelve weeks. Why spend so much time on this phase? The more time you devote to listening, the more clearly you will see a picture of your congregation's current mindset. Allow time to listen during regular Sunday and Wednesday meeting times (or whenever the church family is together). Allow time to hear church members at other church events that are outside the regular meeting times. Allow time to listen to church members in settings that are completely removed from the church grounds. Allow for people to be absent for a week or two, and then to return to the conversation. Allow time for at least a slice of life—both good and bad—to happen to those whose voices you are hearing. A word of warning though; it can be easy to unintentionally exploit what you hear from someone going through a particularly rough passage in his or her marriage. You need to be honest about what you are hearing, but you must also remain objective. You are not making judgments at this point; just listening.

In this phase and phases two and three, the process of gathering information is a bit of a challenge for a couple of reasons. First, we are well-trained in a church context to give the "right" answer. Whether or not it is an honest answer might be a different matter altogether. While gathering information, it is crucial to get honest information. So, you must discover the balance between involving the congregation in the process and the integrity of the process during the discovery phases. If you announce to the congregation who is on the team and what they are listening for, then obviously the conversations around those people both before and after class and worship or out in the community will be different. If your team members stand around the lobby with clipboards asking questions like, "So how's your marriage Steve. Do you and your wife get along well?" you will get the "right" answer but not necessarily the honest answer.

On the other hand, you also do not want this process to be perceived as "Big Brother is watching you." The idea is not to be covert or deceptive. You are not spies. You are not gathering information for the state that can later be used against someone. You are just listening.

The best guide in balancing between congregational involvement and the integrity of the process is common sense. Let the congregation know about your desire to encourage and strengthen healthy marriages for the sake of the kingdom of God. Let them know you have a team who are working to that end. Let them know the leadership of the congregation is fully behind what you are doing. Ask them to pray for God's guidance, the team's progress, and specifically for marriages in the congregation. But being upfront and open about the process does not necessitate spending a month's worth of Sunday morning sermons outlining every detail for the whole congregation. If people are curious and ask, your answer should be straightforward and honest. Don't default to an "only-on-a-need-to-know-basis" answer. If you are dodgy and evasive, your motivations and efforts will be suspect before you ever begin. And, often those who are invested enough to sincerely ask will be strong candidates for future leaders in the ministry.

Most importantly, every member of your team must recognize appropriate confidentiality. A lack of discretion will destroy any credibility you hope to achieve. People who are interested in the process but not currently a part of the team may ask questions about what you are hearing. If any team member names a specific couple, positively or negatively, you have compromised the necessary confidentiality of the process. A strict confidentiality and proper discretion must always be observed, even if talking in general terms that doesn't name names. Although it will eventually be necessary for team members to discuss specific observations, that won't occur until the fourth phase of the process. How you use the information gathered in phases one through three will be detailed in chapter seven, but until you reach that point in the assessment process it is better for a team member to not get into in-depth discussions about what they are hearing so as not to influence other team members' perspectives. So, with that in mind, what exactly are you looking for in the listening phase of this process?

Some guiding thoughts on listening to "the whispers in the hallways"

Each chapter will end with a list of thoughts and questions designed to help your team focus on what they are trying to accomplish at each phase of this process. I am by no means arrogant enough to believe that this list (or the list of thoughts and questions at the end of any other chapter) is a complete list, but these lists are offered as a strong starting point that will at least get you moving in the right direction. I encourage you to expand these lists beyond what is offered here. The unique context of your congregation and your own personal background will always inform how these thoughts and questions are interpreted, as well as what questions will be added or deleted. On many of the statements and questions, I will offer some illustration or commentary to clarify a general intended meaning, but again your own context will define your specific meaning. With that said, let's begin our journey to a proactive marriage ministry that will cast marriage as a calling in the kingdom of God.

What do you hear before and after worship services and Bible classes?

Many segregate their lives into the sacred and the secular. What is permissibly said in the secular context is often taboo in the sacred context. Yet ironically, many subdivide our regular institutional times into times of sacred conversation (during class or in worship) and secular conversation (the transition times before and after class and worship, or at other moments of pause during the sacred times). It is in those brief glimpses of the secular, even on church grounds, that we get a more honest picture of someone's experience of marriage.

How do members talk about marriage in Bible class discussions?

When you study about Sarah preparing a meal for Abraham's three angelic visitors, do comments like "My wife never cooks for me" sound out? Do the ladies speak of their own husbands' sacrificial attitudes when you study Ephesians 5, or are you more likely to hear about "his selfishness"? Although the Bible class time is a sacred time, you can still hear the whispers that reveal underlying thoughts and attitudes. What are the whispers saying?

How do wives speak about their husbands in casual conversation at church sponsored ladies' functions?

Around the card table at a women's retreat or at a social gathering for ladies, do you hear admiration for husbands or do you hear more about their ineptness? When other ladies join the conversation, does the bandwagon move toward negative stories about each lady's husband or does it move toward positive, loving recollections?

How do husbands speak about their wives in casual conversation at church sponsored men's functions?

Sam ministered at a conservative, small-town church. For the most part it was a typical, good church with many committed saints who loved the Lord. One of the big annual events of that church was a men and boys retreat. While overall the retreat was a good time of sports, cards, games, fishing, Christian male bonding, and relaxation, the downfall of this annual event was that it always turned into a wife-bashing weekend. References to "freedom from the old ball and chain" and "a weekend away from the nagging" and far, far worse were commonplace.

"The worst offense," thought Sam, "is that these men have no problem making such rude and insensitive comments about their spouses in front of their own sons. How can he say such rude and callous things about his own boy's mother?!" thought Sam. "Don't they recognize the damage they are doing to their sons' views of the marriage covenant and their sons' relationships with their future wives?"

Is Sam's experience of his church's men and boys retreat typical of conversations at men's events at your congregation?

How are long-term marriages described?

Are you more likely to hear, "How did you stand him for that long?" or "I can really see how she's blessed your life"? Key in on both how those in long-term marriages describe their own relationship, as well as how those commenting on long-term relationships describe a couple's union.

How do those who've been married a long time talk about marriage to those who are not married or have only been married a short time?

Is the language a foreboding, "You just don't know what you're getting yourself into," or is it a tone of joy and hopeful anticipation?

What is the "informal voice" about marriage that comes from the leadership (not an official position or from a teaching or preaching scenario, but in casual conversation and remarks)?

The Main Street Church had a congregational celebration of marriage. They had a wonderful sermon from Ephesians 5 that included a recommitment pledge for married couples in the congregation. The service concluded with an elder standing before the congregation and announcing that he and his wife had been married for almost fifty years. After the applause died down, he "revealed" the secret to a long-term marriage by telling the congregation that their success was entirely due to his "shutting up and doing as he was told." While his impromptu comment drew laughter, this brother failed to recognize what he'd just communicated to the church as a conclusion to their celebration of marriage. Why would any young person in the audience want to pursue a relationship in which he or she could count on being stifled and ordered around for the next half century?

Do wives typically feel like they are honored by their husbands? Do husbands typically feel like they are honored by their wives?

While you cannot ascertain with absolute certainty what someone feels or thinks, by listening you can discern whether it appears a husband or wife feels as if he or she is being treated honorably and respectfully. Sometimes it is noticing if spouses live out 1 Corinthians

13:4-8 with each other—being patient, being kind, not envying or boasting, not being arrogantly prideful, not being rude, or self-serving, not having a quick temper with each other or holding grudges, leading each other toward God's truth while protecting, trusting, and hoping as they faithfully honor their marriage covenant. Although a bit nebulous to define, most of us know a couple that have been married for decades, yet he still opens the door for her; a couple that she patiently waits on him, even as the confusion of Alzheimer's begins to become more apparent.

How often has marriage been praised during this phase of the process?

Is positive conversation about marriage a normal part of your congregational dialogue? You are not so much looking for a tally of how many times good things are said as you are a general tone that permeates the congregation.

How often has marriage been put down (even in a joking manner) during this phase of the process?

A word about humor: There have been times in my marriage that I have wanted to be mad at my wife, usually because of some hurt, real or perceived. Yet, even in the midst of the conflict, I couldn't stay mad at her. Not because of some heartfelt apology, or because she admitted she was wrong and said I was right. It was because we started laughing. More than once in our relationship, Lisa and I have laughed our way beyond the anger of the moment.

Humor is a great component of a joyful marriage. Humor can break tension at just the right moment, make you forget why you're angry, and help you grow closer together. Just about everyone likes to laugh and likes to be around those who can say just the right thing to make them laugh.

In most relationships, teasing is present. It is a way to laugh together, to blow off steam, and maybe even to alert your partner to something you'd be reluctant to talk to them about in a serious manner. However, knowing boundaries when teasing is critical to a healthy marriage. Sometimes, hearing your spouse say the same thing too often begins to hurt. Sometimes, the things you laugh about together in private are received as hurtful and demeaning when said publicly by one spouse or the other. And sometimes, we forget that if the only thing our partner hears is critical teasing without any loving and encouraging words, then the picture painted can very quickly become the reality.

John was stunned when his parents, Rob and Dora, ended their marriage after thirty-plus years. They'd raised their children and should have been looking forward to sharing their golden years together. Instead, Dora was only looking to escape Rob's constant "teasing." For thirty years, he'd relentlessly joked about everything from her appearance to her mannerisms to her cooking to her housekeeping. She was sick of it. It destroyed her self-esteem and made her feel hopeless and unlovable. Rob never realized what he was doing, and Dora never said anything about it because she didn't want to be criticized yet again for "not being able to take a joke."

A marriage without humor would be a sad and pitiable thing. A marriage polluted with humor corrupted by Satan is often worse. Paul's admonition to refrain from "coarse joking" which is out of place for God's holy people (Ephesians 5:4), is not just a warning against dirty jokes, but a warning that Satan can distort "humor." And satanic "humor" can destroy a marriage. How is humor used between spouses in your congregation? Do couples laugh *with* their spouses or *at* their spouses?

Do couples act lovingly toward each other (holding hands, arms around each other, serving each other, tone of voice used, etc.)?

Does the body language of couples in your congregation convey love for each other? I am not suggesting a romanticized "get a room" type of starry-eyed contact, but rather loving and affirming touches and actions. Does he order or ask his wife to refill his drink? Does she try to motivate him through demands or through respect?

How do couples in your congregation perceive the relationship between their marriage and the church?

This is the key question of this book. Does the church offer any spiritual direction for marriage? Do you hear, "This congregation has given us a place to grow as husband and wife" or similar sentiments? Do your members recognize the church as a place that is relevant to a couple's marriage in a real, meaningful way? Do your members recognize the relationship between their marriages and the church within the context of the kingdom of God and their place in the kingdom as a couple? One of the best ways to gather information on this question is through an ethnography study (see below). The ethnography study will help you yield additional information that will relate to all of the questions in this phase as well as questions in other phases, but it allows you to have the additional benefit of a concentrated laser focus on this, the key question of this process.

Using an ethnography study as part of your listening process

What is an ethnography study? Ethnography is the practice of listening to multiple individual stories as a means of hearing an overarching story that points toward a congregational identity. In other words, it is putting the pieces (individual stories) together to see what picture the full puzzle (congregational story) reveals. There are many good books out there on what ethnography is, how to use an ethnography study, and what you should expect an ethnography study to yield. (My personal favorite is Mary Clark Moschella's *Ethnography as a Pastoral Practice: An Introduction,* Pilgrim Press, 2008).

In my congregation, we used an ethnography study to determine whether or not community life at our congregation honestly impacted a couple's marriage. While a book like Moschella's will explain a more detailed process, in order to illustrate the value of this process, below is a synopsis of what we did and the results it yielded.

First, we selected the couples we wanted to interview. The couples were chosen to give a representative sampling of the whole congregation. Age, ethnicity, family dynamics, and various other factors that we determined to be important to our church community life were carefully considered. In a smaller congregation, it might actually be possible to interview a majority of couples in the church, but in a congregation our size (nearly a thousand members), the logistics of finding enough interviewers and compiling the data at the end of the project would have been overwhelming. So, a representative sampling was a more feasible route.

Next, we crafted the questions that each interviewer would ask the couples being interviewed. Every couple interviewed was asked the exact same set of questions in order to strengthen the validity of the findings. The questions were carefully written so as to avoid simple "yes" or "no" type answers. We were also careful to not ask leading questions that might make our findings lean toward a pre-supposed conclusion. The questions allowed those interviewed to share their past and present reality, but also to unleash their imagination and dreams for couples and their participation in our congregation as participation in the kingdom of God.

All the interviews were done independently of each other, and most lasted about one to two hours. The interviewers were gifted listeners, hearing the couples' stories and resisting the temptation to constantly interject their own experiences or take over the conversation. Whatever method the interviewer used to remember the interview, whether audio recording or notes, was made obvious to the couple being interviewed. Also, the interviewers assured the couples of appropriate levels of confidentiality.

Once all the interviews were finished, the interviewers gathered for a few hours and discussed their findings. Although each couple had a unique and interesting life story, we began to notice common elements emerging; elements that related to each couple's experience of marriage within the context of their involvement with our church community.

From the ethnography project, we discovered five elements that continually appeared. At least four of the five appeared in every couple's story, and all five appeared in several interviews. The five things we discovered were, first, a greater desire for relational authenticity. All of the couples interviewed recognized the "church face" stigma and longed for something different. Second, there was recognition of the need for better and earlier education about marriage as a kingdom calling. The past methods were inconsistent and failed to connect marriage to kingdom participation. Third, there was a desire for mentoring. Couples wanted to connect to other couples, particularly older couples, who had experience and knowledge from which they could glean. Fourth, there was also a call for slowing down, putting less on the church calendar, and creating a church culture that doesn't create a guilt-complex if we don't attend various activities. The culture's addiction to busyness was splitting couples and families apart in the name of ministry. And finally, there was a desire for relationships that mean something. While there was a broad range of relationships within the congregation, many couples did not sense a depth of relationship they could call upon during times of crisis.

A word of warning; if you choose to make an ethnography study a part of your listening process, expect some people, perhaps even some leading members of the congregation, to challenge your findings. From the moment we presented our findings that defined an overarching story, we encountered resistance from some quarters. Some were quick to defend the status quo, particularly the busyness of the church calendar, denying its effects on couples and families in the congregation. Others attacked the validity of the study, saying we needed a larger sampling before they would believe our findings. A few just dismissed it as a waste of time since any real change was, in their opinion, unnecessary and probably unlikely to happen. Change is uncomfortable, and it is always easier to criticize efforts which highlight the need for change than it is to actually make the changes. It is always easier to be reactive later than proactive now.

If you choose to pursue an ethnography study, it will add additional time and effort for your team, but the results gained will be invaluable. As with every other question asked in this part of the process, it is extremely important to remember that if you choose to pursue an ethnography study, the key is to listen. You might not like what you hear. You might not agree with a particular couple's perception of marriage or the relationship between matrimony and church life. But you are only listening. You are not seeking to influence anything at this point.

Chapter 4

Phase 2: Analyzing the Landscape

At the church where I grew up, ninety-five percent of married couples were in their first and only marriage. Of the remaining five percent, the majority were widows or widowers who remarried in their golden years. Only one or two couples were divorced and remarried, and they were easy to identify because the children had different last names.

Was the church I grew up in really that way? There are a lot of reasons it could have been. It was a different time. There was more of a stigma on divorce back then, particularly since we lived in a small rural town of about five thousand. And, in our little congregation of two hundred, everybody pretty well knew everybody else's business, so no one wanted to add the shame of divorce to the list of things for gossip fodder. But was it really that way?

While the church I grew up in was probably very different then from my current congregation now (though I doubt that home church is much different today), it probably was not quite as pristine as I remember it. We all bring a set of assumptions with us to our church family. Whether you are still in the congregation you were born into or you move to a new church home every few years, you see married couples in a particular light, based on previous church experience, personal experience, and a slew of other factors. For me, when I meet a new couple I automatically assume they are in their first marriage until I have some reason to believe otherwise. I probably think that way because I am not from a divorced family and I have never been divorced myself (and of course because of the perfect little church I remember from my childhood). I am not making any kind of statement about divorce and remarriage one way or the other. I am just sharing what informs my most familiar context for evaluating other situations; what informs my "default setting," if you will.

So, does it matter if a couple is in their first marriage or not? Does it matter if my assumptions are correct or not? Well, yes and no. It doesn't make a difference in the way I will treat them personally. My calling is to love God and to love my neighbor as myself, so I treat them as I believe Jesus would treat them. But it does make a difference in how that couple will exist, function, and participate in the community life of the church. Just like any other family situation, blended families bring a specific set of gifts, needs, circumstances, and problems to the table. How a person who went through a bitter divorce hears a sermon is different from how a happily married person hears it. A blended family's participation in church life is impacted if one of the children is in a different town every other weekend visiting with the non-custodial parent. Someone in a second marriage can stand before the church as a model of forgiveness, grace, and mercy in how she treats her ex. The list goes on and on of ways that, yes, it does matter. How sermons are preached, how classes are taught, how the calendar is planned, what types of emphases different ministries carry—every aspect of community life within a church is affected by the members of the body to which a given congregation is ministering. More about this will be discussed in chapter eight, but for now, suffice it to say, it does matter.

In this phase of the process, you will look at the current state of marriage in your congregation. Now at this point, many will say "I know the current state of marriage in my congregation! That's why I picked up this book." But, are you sure you know your congregation, or are you projecting your own set of assumptions on couples in the congregation? And even if you do feel you have a good concept of the divorce and remarriage situation are you as certain about other areas of matrimony that affect the landscape of your congregation? Ask yourself the following questions:

- Who has been married the longest at this congregation?
- Who is the most recent marriage at this congregation?
- What percent of your members are in their first marriage?
- Have more couples here been married over 15 years or less than 15 years? 20 years? 25 years? What number is the dividing line for the majority of couples in your congregation?
- How many couples in this congregation have been married over 50 years?
- What percent of couples in this church are part of a blended family?
- Have any couples divorced but later reconciled?
- What couple has the most children?
- How many couples have or currently are seeing a marriage counselor?
- How many engaged couples are there?

How did you do answering these questions? Are you sure of your answers?

In this phase of the process, the marriage ministry leadership team will gather data that will give a realistic picture of the church's current marriage landscape. This stage will strip away the assumptions you are carrying with you and clarify the reality of your church's situation as opposed to your "gut perceptions."

Some guiding thoughts on discovering the marriage landscape of your congregation

As with the previous stage of the process, this stage is a means of listening to the congregation, just from a different angle. This stage of the process can take anywhere from a few weeks to a few months, depending on how adamantly your team pursues it. Because this stage is more attuned to research and statistics, it will not be everyone's cup of tea. However, it is likely that you have a few people on your team who love this type of thing. To those people, it is a challenge and a passion to dig through old records, gather information, and to know things with as much certainty as humanly possible. While this stage can be done at the same time that you are listening to the whispers in the hallways, be sure that team members give full attention to both phases. For those who embrace this type of task, it is fine to let them take the lead, but the entire team needs to participate so as to have a stake in every stage of the process. There is a temptation for those on your team who favor the work generated by phase two to play to their natural strengths and neglect phase one. But don't give in to the temptation. Everyone on the team needs to be as engaged as possible on each phase, so that when you move into phase four (chapter 7), all your team members will have an equal and informed voice.

Below is a list of thoughts and questions designed to help your team map out an accurate landscape of marriage within your congregation. As with the first phase, this list is offered as a strong starting point to get you moving in the right direction. The unique context of your congregation will always inform what information will be added or deleted as you seek to better know your church family.

On a final note for this phase, be sure that you have the most reliable sources possible as you gather this information. Everything from old church bulletins to the computer database in the church office to direct communication from church members will be necessary to gain accurate information and clarify the picture you are seeking to put together. Remember, we all carry assumptions, so information gathered from members may at times be conflicting and need to be verified. That doesn't mean anyone is seeking to provide false information. It is just the nature of how we interpret our community around us.

What is the total number of married couples in your congregation?

Whether you are looking at first marriages, second marriages, divorced and remarried, or widowed and remarried, this is your starting point for assessing the relationship between couples and the church.

What is the total number of people who never married, divorced but have not remarried, and widows or widowers who have not remarried?

As you begin to look at the relationship between those who are single and those who are married in your congregation, it becomes important to recognize what section of your congregation might be looking toward marriage in the future, as well as singles who have previous personal experience (good or bad) with marriage.

How many married couples are active in the congregational life of the church?

This is not an inclusion/exclusion question, but a means of considering the connection between marriage and church. It is also a way of thinking about who is on the fringe, who is playing the "church face" game, and what, if anything, the church does to plug couples into Kingdom calling and living. As you consider how active couples are, perhaps the more significant question is, are they active *together* in the congregational life of the church.

How many couples are you aware of that are currently in a marriage crisis (beyond normal stresses and season of life issues)?

This question is a bit nebulous and requires some judgment calls because *your* normal stress or season of life issue is not the same as *my* normal. My wife Lisa and I had a two-year stretch in which I had a serious car wreck, then shortly after that my mother-in-law died. Within a few months both my mother and Lisa's father had hip replacement surgery at the same time, both of them requiring additional care from us. Lisa and I were served with papers for a lawsuit because of the wreck. I started a doctoral program that required me to rearrange my schedule significantly as well as traveling out of state for several weeks each year. Our son had to have eye surgery. I had a massive head injury that landed me in the hospital for a few days with lingering complications afterwards. My wife's dad had to have his other hip replaced and developed heart issues. And, we still had all the normal stresses of working and caring for three small children. For us, it was not a pleasant two-year stretch.

Thankfully, during that time our church family was a blessing to us, at times bringing food or taking care of our kids, and constantly praying for us. Although we were often grieved, tired, frazzled, scared, confused, and frustrated, Lisa and I never really considered ourselves to be in a crisis, especially in regard to our marriage. Some couples face similar situations, but because of their unique circumstances, it puts their marriage in jeopardy. Others face far worse than Lisa and I did and do just as well or better than we did. Some couples encounter what we would consider much milder stresses but because those stresses are part of a compilation of other factors, it sends that couple reeling.

So what determines if a stressor is just a bump on the marriage road or a seemingly insurmountable barrier? It depends on the couple you are considering. Everything from the couple's unique background, to their current circumstances, to their maturity level, to their life history, to their family support network factors into the equation. The safest route is to simply ask when major life changes happen. What might be nothing to me and Lisa might be a colossal marriage-testing trial to another couple. Ask. Don't just assume every other couple will encounter stressors the same way you and your spouse do.

How many couples in our congregation are in their first marriage? Second? Third or later?

It is a mistake to assume a "one size fits all" definition of what marriage and a family should look like. The traditional nuclear family of husband, wife, and their shared offspring is no longer nearly as predominant as it was decades ago. In most congregations, the population of blended families is rapidly growing and will continue to grow. It cannot be an overlooked minority.

As you explore this question, what you find can become a minefield of complexity. Not only will you find blended families, you might find blended-blended families in which a person is married for a third or fourth time with children by more than one previous spouse. You will find situations in which it is her first marriage, but his second, or his second, but her fourth. How do you distinguish between a second marriage due to divorce and a second marriage due to the death of a spouse? If someone previously divorced and remarried, but their former spouse has since died, do you classify that person as a divorcee or as a widow?

It is a worthwhile endeavor to try and figure it all out since the statistical rate of success declines with each subsequent marriage. But don't let this pursuit get you bogged down to the point you feel overwhelmed by the myriad number of situations that exist within the congregation. As a good rule of thumb, if either spouse has been divorced, you can normally consider both as living in a divorce and remarriage. Regardless if it is his first marriage and her second, as a couple they are still navigating the effects of divorce together—dealing with an ex, working through shared custody of children, coping with emotional responses, and the like. As you unravel this knot, this particular aspect of the marriage landscape of your congregation will strongly determine how you will structure and carry out ministries and where you will concentrate resources.

How does this congregation's divorce rate compare to the national average?

As noted before, you must be careful when dealing with statistics, as they are easily manipulated. Make sure your numbers are coming from a reliable resource, such as the United States government's vital statistics listed at www.cdc.gov. If you want to carry your investigation a step further, local agencies can provide divorce stats for your specific state or town.

How old is the longest (still ongoing) marriage in your congregation? What is the most recent marriage?

Is a long-term marriage an anomaly or commonplace? Are new marriages frequent or a rare happening?

Of the total number of couples in your church, how many have been married: 0-5 years, 6 to 10 years, 11 to 15 years, 16 to 20 years, 21 to 25 years, 26 to 30 years, 31 to 35 years, 36 to 40 years, 41 to 45 years, 46 to 50 years, over 50 years?

Each phase of marriage brings with it unique joys and unique challenges. The more familiar you are with the exact demographics of your married couples, the better equipped you will be to minister to them and afford opportunities for kingdom participation. Knowing where couples actually are will assist with planning and allow you to utilize your resources more competently. Everything from the depth and breadth of a mentoring program to the lessons most needed for a weekend couples' getaway is determined by this information.

Looking back at the last ten years, has the number of failed marriages at your congregation increased, decreased or remained unchanged? To what do you attribute this change or lack of change?

Everything from urbanization to advances in technology to a major employer in an area closing down can affect marriages. Has anything happened to cause a shift either in the physical or psychological makeup of your community that has had ripple effects within the church community? Sometimes those shifts come fast and radically and other times they come slow and subtly.

Was there a period in the church's history in which there were significantly more or less divorces? If so, to what would this be attributed?

Very likely, the changing cultural influence on the church and decline of the social stigma attached to divorce has allowed for an increase in failed marriages from years gone by. But, other factors also can affect a specific time period in a congregation's history. From time to time, communities decline and new temptations are introduced. At other times, those same communities are cleaned up through renewal, removal of lascivious businesses, crackdowns on prostitution and addictive vices, and in a number of other ways. New employers or a robust economy can renew hope and reduce daily stress. Times of political peace and unity can contribute to marital satisfaction. Natural disasters, such as a tornado, or flood, or earthquake, or hurricane can have a profound effect on marriages as it can completely obliterate the normal routines of life and cause unbelievable levels of stress. Whatever the external circumstances, negative or positive, the more fully you understand what triggers stresses and marital dissatisfaction, the more equipped you are to help couples walk through those times.

What is the history of appointed and/or volunteer leadership positions in your church as those positions relate to marriage?

Have you ever had a minister who was divorced? What about an elder? A deacon? A volunteer in a significant lead position? Are those in second or later marriages permitted to teach Bible classes in your congregation? Can they lead prayers, serve communion, or participate in any aspect of public worship? Can a divorced person organize a church fellowship meal? Work on the church computer system? Clean the auditorium? Is there a dividing line, a perceived level of authority or leadership, where someone who is divorced is no longer allowed to serve?

Has this always been the case in your congregation or was there a change at some point? If so, what caused the change? Was a divorced person in a second marriage allowed to serve as a deacon because his first marriage was deemed a scripturally justifiable divorce? Was a divorced woman allowed to teach a Bible class because she was an elder's daughter? Did the change in who could or could not serve occur due to personal involvement from a church leader or his family, or was the change a unilateral move that came from study of God's Word? Understanding the history of marriage and your church in regard to leadership positions is critical to really seeing the marriage landscape of your congregation.

Looking over the edge

Years ago, my wife and I were blessed enough to stand looking over the edge of Waimea Canyon in Kauai, Hawaii with our dear friends Mike and Cindy. As we stood on the precipice, I was awed by the panoramic majesty of God's creation. Lisa marveled at the rainbow bursting forth from the mist that continually rose from the canyon's floor. Mike was keenly aware of the three helicopters that slowly made their way around the canyon, loaded with tourists who could afford a closer view of the canyon walls than the four of us could. And Cindy noticed the shimmering crystal blue waters lapping on the edge of the bottom of the canyon.

Although we all stood at the same vantage point and saw the same thing, our individual foci were on different aspects of the same view. I'm sure the dozens and dozens of other visitors to the island who surrounded us that beautiful June afternoon noticed other things that we either minimized or missed altogether. Everything from rock formations to the position of the sun to the annoying wild chickens that seemed to be running around everywhere, different things caught each person's attention or demanded different levels of priority. And, everything from the time of day to the season of the year to how cloudy it might be affects how visitors before and after us focused on the canyon.

As you paint the landscape of marriage in your congregation, you will create a powerful picture. Even though everyone will see the same set of facts, different members of your team will deem various parts of that picture as more important or less important than you do based on their individual backgrounds and experiences. Regardless of one's individual perspective on the information gathered, this phase represents a second voice about marriage in your congregation. In the next chapter we will explore the third voice of marriage present at every church.

Chapter 5

Phase 3: The Formal Voice of Marriage

The speed limit on Interstate 24 drops from 70 miles per hour to 55 miles per hour just past the Harding Road exit as you move toward downtown Nashville. Somewhere on that little stretch of highway an amazing paradox happens. The speed limit changes, but it really doesn't change. Or does it? The sign says 55, but I'm not sure I have ever observed anyone slowing down to 55. The flow of traffic continues along at 70 miles per hour (or faster!). Yet, if a Nashville police officer or Tennessee state trooper appears, that officer has every right and reason to give someone a ticket for breaking the law. At our congregation we have one such officer. He once said the most frequent question he is asked is "Why me? No one else obeys the speed limit through here, so why pull me over? Why me?" His answer is simply, "Why not you?" The state has declared the expectations for someone driving on I-24 through that particular area. Whether those expectations are followed or not, whether or not it is a reasonable speed limit for that area, whether someone gets caught breaking the law or not is all a moot point. Fifty-five miles per hour is the stated law.

In every congregation, there are formal laws of marriage. At this point I am not talking exclusively about biblical interpretations about marriage (we'll get to that later), but what does the church believe its public face of marriage to be? What are you telling your membership and the larger community around you that you believe and practice when it comes to marriage (whether your own couples observe it or not)? What are the "formal voices of marriage" in your congregation? The formal voices are the official positions that your church takes regarding marriage and how those positions are communicated to the congregation. Formal positions are represented by both *what* is said and *who* says what. These things are not always written down, but can come from positional authority.

What do I mean by "positional authority?" The preaching minister or elder's words spoken from the pulpit or in a Bible class setting carry weight, even if what is said is not intended to be an "official" statement of faith and practice. By virtue of who they are and the authority and trust the church community places on them, their words mean something. By the same token, where people of authority speak also carries weight. Words spoken in a casual conversation in a diner on a Friday night do not always carry the same weight as words spoken from the pulpit on a Sunday morning, even if they are the exact same words. The degrees of authority carried by various people will be different from congregation to congregation. A new minister might not yet carry the same voice of authority as a Bible class teacher who has taught for forty years. A well-liked elder's wife might speak more authoritatively than all the deacons in a church.

In the third phase of this process, the leadership team will listen to the third voice of marriage in your congregation, the formal voice of marriage. How is this done? By looking at the church's publicly communicated face of marriage. This can be an exceptionally revealing endeavor, highlighting the "law" of marriage present in the church. It becomes even more interesting as you become aware of whether or not the formal voice of marriage in your congregation matches the "spirit" of marriage you are hearing from the whispers in the hallway.

Some guiding thoughts on hearing the publicly communicated voice of marriage at your congregation

As with the previous two stages of the process, this stage is a means of listening to the congregation from yet another angle. This stage of the process can take anywhere from a few weeks to a few months. Like phases one and two, this stage can be done simultaneously, but be careful not to overload your team members. Be sure that team members give full attention to all three phases for the same reason mentioned before. When you move into phase four, you will want all your team members to have an equal and informed voice.

Below is a list of thoughts and questions designed to help your team know what to look for when assessing your church's publicly communicated voice of marriage. As you proceed with this phase, you will undoubtedly notice other ways your congregation is or is not saying something about marriage. Remember, at this point you are still not seeking to change anything, just listen and observe.

What does a walk-through of our church building show about our regard or disregard for marriage?

There is both a "who" and a "what" that reveals the existing formal voice (or law) of marriage at your congregation. We are often more aware of the "who" than we are of the "what." Consider some of the things your church might be communicating about marriage based on the "what" of your congregation's physical presence. Is there a bulletin board dedicated to marriage matters? Is there a section in your church library that deals with marriage, and if so, how current and relevant are the books or videos? Are there pictures or posters on the walls that say anything about marriage? Do class advertisements communicate anything? If you have a tract rack or periodicals rack, is there any literature about marriage? Visually, is there anything about your auditorium, classrooms, foyer, fellowship hall, or other parts of your building that communicates a view of marriage (positive or negative)? What does your place of worship say? I am not advocating that your building should be constantly decorated like a wedding chapel, but just encouraging you to honestly observe and evaluate.

Is there a "marriage presence" on your church website? In your church bulletin? In other publications or modes of information distribution?

Along with what your church building says physically, what do your written communications say about marriage? Does your church website say something about what your congregation believes about marriage or have links to other websites that can benefit couples? What about your church bulletin or newsletter? At my congregation, we have a section on the front cover of the bulletin titled "Family Matters." It takes up about one fourth of the front page and offers biblically-based reflections, insights, advice, encouragement, commendations, and challenges for our church family. On the first week of each month "Family Matters" is about marriage. On the second week it is about parenting teens. The third week relates to the whole family structure. The fourth week is about parenting younger children. And, if there is a fifth week, it deals with aging and issues faced by senior citizens. Undoubtedly, after several years of having this on the front of our bulletin, to some it has become "just another thing." But, whether it is eagerly awaited each week or not, it has become a recognizable, identifying mark for my congregation.

What is written or printed by your congregation about marriage? Is it a consistent presence or a random happenstance?

How often is marriage mentioned from the pulpit and in what context?

After I preached a sermon on the kingdom calling of marriage, a gentleman in the congregation came up to me and said, "Congratulations, I think that is the first time I've ever heard a sermon on marriage that didn't try to make it all a big joke." How is marriage broadcast from your church's pulpit? Are sermon illustrations involving marriage usually demeaning to wives? Insulting to husbands? Negative? Or, do they illustrate mutual admiration and respect, forgiveness and grace, God-filled humor and joy, and other virtues that communicate a relationship blessed by Christ? Discovering the answer to this question may require interviewing the preaching minister and/or listening to a couple of years worth of sermon tapes. As you do this, be careful not to put the preaching minister into an uncomfortable, defensive position. You're listening and discovering, not passing judgment.

What is the main minister's "rule of thumb" on performing marriages? Do other ministers and/or church leaders share his viewpoint?

Regardless of the specific titles your congregation uses, in most churches someone is regarded as the lead or main minister. Typically, it is the preaching minister due to the visibility of the pulpit, but it might also be the minister with the most longevity at the congregation. Whoever it is, what "rule of thumb" does that minister use when asked to perform a wedding?

Some ministers refuse to perform a wedding unless they personally approve of the marriage. Some won't do it if it is a second or later marriage, regardless of the circumstances. Some will marry anyone, seeing their participation in the process as an avenue for sharing Christ with the couple. How clear cut is the main minister's criteria for performing a wedding ceremony? Is that criteria communicated to the congregation? Does that criteria flow from a personal theology of marriage, church polity, a leadership directive, or from somewhere else? How free do other ministers and church leaders feel in breaking with the main minister's "rule of thumb"?

How often are there Bible classes devoted specifically to marriage matters?

Are classes that help couples to have a more God-centered marriage the norm or the exception at your congregation? To what level have you explored different formats and different resources?

What is the rationale behind how often marriage is mentioned in classes, sermons, or other formats?

This question strikes at the heart of whether your congregation is reactive or proactive. Is the intersection of marriage and church intentional and purposeful or is it incidental and random? If you have a spring quarter marriage class because you always have a spring quarter marriage class, that is okay, but is there more to it than just filling a slot on a teaching schedule? Is the annual sermon on marriage a habitual token lesson, or is it deliberate? And how much communication is there between the preaching minister, the education director, and other church leaders to determine how and when marriage matters are taught and studied?

Is marriage addressed in the preschool and children's curriculums? If so, how often and in what context? At what age does it begin? What, if anything, is said about marriage at each age level?

Children are like sponges, absorbing anything and everything they see, hear, and experience. What are they absorbing about marriage in your Bible classes? From the earliest years, are they being trained to see marriage as something godly? Are they being trained to see marriage as something connected to the community life of the church or as a social construct that we've Christianized? What are they being told about who created marriage and the purpose of marriage? Obviously, there is appropriate information for each age level, but in an overall context, how integrated are teachings about marriage in your preschool curriculum?

At my church, for the last twenty years that the preschool class curriculum has studied Isaac and Rebekah, Ms. Sally has held a pre-school wedding. Each year, on a specific Wednesday night, with full decorations and pomp, her precious little four and five year old students pretend to get married. A minister or elder talks to each little couple about marriage and what it means to serve someone else (on their level, of course) and then pronounces them "pretend husband and wife." While this one event is not the end-all for teaching children about marriage, it is an annual reminder of the importance of teaching and reinforcing these lessons now, knowing they are soaking it all up.

How is marriage handled in the teen Bible classes? What resources are available for teens regarding dating and marriage? What conversations are developing, and how is the leadership addressing them?

When I was ten years old, my family hosted the December teen devotional in our home. Though I was not quite a teen myself, it was at my house so I got to sit in with my two older brothers and all their friends. Since it was December, our youth minister led us in "Silent Night, Holy Night." After the song was finished, I promptly raised my hand and, much to the utter embarrassment of my brothers, I asked the youth minister in front of all my brothers' friends, "What's a virgin?" We'd just sung "'Round yon virgin, mother and child," so I needed to know what a virgin was. Maybe I was a sheltered or naïve child, but children today see, hear, and know so much more at an earlier and earlier age. So how equipped are your church's teen classes to handle this overload of information and contextualize Christian marriage into the culture's message about relationships?

I am a fan of True Love Waits and other abstinence programs like it, but what is the context of the message your teen classes teach about sexuality in regard to marriage? Is the only message they hear "Don't do it until you're married," or is sex viewed as a gift created by God, but placed within healthy, holy boundaries? Are messages that address dating, sex, and other aspects of marriage presented from a negative, "No! No! No!" standpoint, or a positive "Look what God created for you" perspective? As their hormones rage, do your teen classes tempt them toward a stronger desire for forbidden fruit or guide them toward anticipating a godly relationship?

Does your teen curriculum address divorce? Many of your teens may be facing tough questions and have jaded or even faith-shaking experiences of their parents' marriage falling apart. Are your teen Bible classes equipped and even proactive in addressing those questions?

Does your church give parents the tools they need to guide their teens toward healthy Christian marriages? Does your church equip adults to mentor and interact with teens in a way that will help them to see God's calling for marriage?

Does the formal voice of marriage at your congregation seem to always be presented from a negative stance?

Sometimes a prohibitive message is necessary, timely, and beneficial. But if the negative is all that is ever broadcast, what is the tone of marriage your congregation presents to the larger community of which you are a part?

Is pre-marital counseling provided for couples? Does the church require pre-marital counseling for couples using the church building for their wedding? Why or why not?

Many churches provide pre-marital counseling. Even churches that do not offer clinical counseling will offer pastoral counseling. If your church provides it, what curriculum or resources are used? Are you familiar with resources such as PREPARE/ENRICH or other assessment tools? Who does the counseling? Do those who do the counseling receive any training? One minister's four hour pre-marital counseling consists of talking to a couple for a couple of hours about whatever they want to talk about and then telling them to "go watch that fire movie" (he is referring to *Fireproof*), with no follow up afterwards. While there may be some good that comes from those sessions, is that the extent of what your congregation wants to do to help couples prepare for a lifetime commitment?

My congregation requires a minimum of four hours with either one of our ministers or with a competent counselor before our elders will let our building be used for a wedding. Sadly, most couples from outside our congregation who choose to use our building are inclined to want to wait until less than six weeks before the wedding to schedule the counseling. Then they scramble to find some way to cram in four hours of sessions amid wedding planning, work schedules, and all the other distractions of life. Regardless of how the participating couple views the counseling, the policies you have in place say something about your congregation's view of the relationship between the church and married couples.

Are professional counseling services available for couples in distress?

Some congregations are blessed enough to have full time counselors, either on the church payroll or through a cooperative program. Most, however, are not. Does your congregation have a way to refer couples who need professional counseling?

Are church leaders (elders, ministers, church staff, deacons, lead volunteers, etc.) encouraged or required to have an annual visit with a professional marriage counselor for a marriage health check-up?

This is where the rubber meets the road. Many church leaders balk at the suggestion of having an annual marriage health check-up and some downright rebel at the idea of it being mandatory. Whether we want to admit it or not, there is a strong stigma associated with going to counseling. Undoubtedly, many leaders will say, "We've been married thirty (or forty, or fifty, or more) years and everything is fine. We don't need to see a counselor!" Yet, what does it communicate to the congregation when the leadership hedges at insuring their own marital health? And, being married to a minister's wife, I know there is a level of stress that falls on a church leader's spouse that those spouses often feel they cannot openly discuss. Whether you intend to or not, you might be perpetuating the "church face" culture within your own leadership.

If the leadership does not model strong, healthy marriages, you cannot expect the rest of the church family to follow suit. Lord willing, a yearly check-up will take a little time, create some healthy conversation, and result in an "all's fine" diagnosis. And if a leadership couple does discover there's a problem, wouldn't it have been a far worse thing to have failed to ask?

Do couples know where they can go to find marriage resources (church library, bulletin board with articles, section in the weekly bulletin, links from the church website, etc.)?

Over and over, after pointing couples to a given resource I hear, "We didn't know there was anything like this out there."

If, after reviewing what your church currently offers, you decide it's time to begin or expand the resources available, here are a couple of things to remember. First, there are plenty of Christian marriage resources, but knowing what to recommend takes real discernment. Many resources are based on pop psychology that uses Christianized language, but are light on any real biblical foundations. Some are strong on "feel good" solutions that sound promising but have no real spiritual depth. Others offer solid theory, but are not nearly as practical for the realities of living in a fallen world. The range from really good to really bad material is staggering. Constantly review, update, critique, and utilize what is available.

Second, as you utilize different materials, most people have a tendency to gravitate toward a particular favorite. Whether it is an author, a video series, a web site's postings, or whatever else, usually one or two specific resources will fall in line with our own personal view and experience of marriage more than others. While it's okay to have favorites, be careful not to let one resource become your only resource. No one resource can cover every scenario, and no one resource speaks to every couple the same.

Does your church sponsor or participate in marriage enrichment activities or events outside of normal Bible class times?

Whether it is couples' retreats, marriage seminars, or other events designed to refocus couples on Christ and each other, is anything happening in your congregation? If so, how often? If it happened in the past, but isn't currently, what has changed? Does your church family see a benefit to disconnecting from the rush of life for extended times to allow couples to refocus on their shared kingdom purpose?

Are new marriages publically celebrated by your church?

Most churches recognize recent weddings in the bulletin or perhaps in the Sunday morning announcements, in a Bible class, or on the website, but do you celebrate new marriages? How a congregation celebrates new marriages may be as simple as the preaching minister or an elder offering a special prayer for the couple. It might be a reaffirmation with the whole congregation of the church's theology of marriage (see below for more on that). It may be something as elaborate as a periodic worship service or designated time in a worship service that newly married couples receive a special blessing. Does your congregation celebrate new marriages or do you just recognize them?

Are significant anniversaries publicly celebrated?

On January 1, 2011, Nathan and Evelyn Graham marked their 65th wedding anniversary. To say we had a party to celebrate would be an understatement. With the help of their children and family, after evening worship on the first Sunday night of that year, over four hundred members of the Graham's church family came together to celebrate. Although it was the Grahams' anniversary, we all took ownership of it. We celebrated it as a milestone for the whole church community. We realized that between divorce, death, and the trend toward couples marrying later in life, the likelihood of seeing many other couples reach this monumental occasion would be an incredibly rare occurrence. The Grahams' anniversary was a powerful time for our congregation to talk about marriage, commitment, covenant, and Christ-centered love and living. Parents pointed their children toward the Grahams as a model of what Christian marriage is supposed to look like.

While most churches will not see many (if any) 65th marriage anniversaries, do you use significant anniversaries as times of renewal and reminder for the relationship between couples and the church? As noted in the question above, there is certainly a difference between recognizing and celebrating. While it would not necessarily be practical and beneficial to celebrate every anniversary in a major public way, there are some anniversaries that deserve attention. Many churches note 25th and 50th anniversaries, either through Bible classes, in the bulletin, or possibly from the pulpit, but most churches neglect 1st anniversaries. In fact, sometimes couples are embarrassed to admit they are only celebrating a first through fifth anniversary because they know all they will hear are comments like, "just you wait" or "you don't know anything yet." While a young couple might still have a lot to learn, churches need to at least recognize the earliest anniversaries, letting that recognition and/or celebration be a source of encouragement for young couples. And, if the encouragement and congratulations come from older couples, it can mean so much more to those just starting on their marriage journey.

Is there any type of marriage small groups meeting?

Whether church organized or self-formed, meeting during regular institutional times or on a periodic weekday schedule, couples' small groups can provide an excellent avenue for accountability, transparency, prayer, and especially a couple's connection into the church family. There is a multitude of ways to organize and carry out marriage small groups. Is your congregation pursuing any of them?

What is your church's theology of marriage?

This question is the heart, soul, and foundation of what your marriage ministry is and will become. This will be of central importance as you move into the fifth stage of this process. In fact, this particular question is important enough that the entire next chapter will be devoted to it.

Chapter 6

Finding a Theology of Marriage

What do you think of when someone says "theology"? For most people, theology is an enigmatic concept. Some see theology as what academic eggheads with advanced degrees endlessly discuss with no real understanding of what life is like in the real world. Others see it as something daunting and intimidating that is "best left to people smarter than me." While there are some who enjoy the challenge of working through a theological issue, far more feel the pursuit of theology, at least in the way it is normally viewed, is an endlessly unfruitful struggle that drains time and resources.

Most churches that are concerned about their marriages want to bypass the theology and go straight to programming. It is always easier to be reactive and look for the quick fix. But, just like building a house, if you put it up too quickly without making sure there's a firm foundation underneath, you might get something that looks pretty for a season, but what lasting effect will it have for your congregation? Didn't Jesus have something to say about skipping over a solid foundation? Finding your congregation's theology of marriage is the single most important part of the entire process. It is the solid foundation from which every other aspect of your congregation's treatment of marriage will flow. If you want to have Christian marriages within your congregation, then you must begin with a biblically-informed view of marriage. You must discern a theology of marriage for your congregation.

Still, the idea of coming up with a foundational theology for your congregation might seem frightening or overwhelming. Let's take a moment to demystify the process of developing theology. In simplest terms, theology is the place where faith intersects with the human condition. Undoubtedly, there is both good theology and bad theology. If your theology ignores the actual human condition, then it will become nothing more than a "pie in the sky" illusion, an unobtainable quest that endlessly taunts you. But, on the other side of that equation, if we allow the human condition to dictate our theology, then we don't believe in God. At least we don't believe in the God of Scripture whose thoughts are not our thoughts and whose ways are not our ways (Isaiah 55:8-9). If the human condition completely drives our theology, then our god is much more akin to the Greek gods or the other pantheons of pagan gods who display all the sinful shortcomings of humanity.

So what is a good theology then? The goal of good theology is the balance between striving for the ideal that God puts before us while engaging the reality of living in a fallen world. It is uncompromisingly and unapologetically living for God, but living in grace, mercy, humility, and forgiveness. It is accepting the invitation to live the resurrection life, acting as God's instruments for reconciling the world back to Him through Christ (2 Corinthians 5), and being salt and light to point others toward Christ (Matthew 5:13-16).

"Okay," you say, "so how do we do that?" First, recognize that discerning theology is not as unfamiliar as you think. In fact, we all discern theology every day. It is part of our daily decision-making process; deciding between what we believe to be right and what we believe to be wrong based on our faith and our understanding of the Word of God. We make theologically-based decisions individually. Should I say that? Should I go there? Should I be watching this? How can I help him? Am I being honest with her? What is God calling me to do? And, we make theologically-based decisions with others. What is the right thing for us to do as a family? In what way can this church serve? How can we work together to feed the hungry? What do we believe about this matter? Can we stand behind that action?

Next, discuss this with the leadership of your congregation to see if there is already a well-defined and articulated theology of marriage. But be specific about what you are asking for. Many churches have a well articulated theology of divorce and remarriage. These congregations are quick to give you a definitive answer about what does and does not constitute a proper marriage "in God's eyes." Typically, what that entails is a list of prohibitions for the person who finds himself or herself in a second or later marriage. It might be the divorced person can't stand up front during public worship, or can't teach a Bible class. Perhaps he or she can't serve on a planning committee or chaperone a youth event. Depending on the congregation, the list of prohibitions could be quite lengthy. In some cases, the person who is divorced and remarried might hear that he or she is only allowed to sit on the pew and drop money in the collection plate. In extreme cases, a church might even condemn the divorced person to eternal damnation with no hope of redemption.

This book is not about divorce and remarriage. Whatever perspective of divorce and remarriage you embrace, it is important to have a well-grounded, biblically-based, culturally-relative theology regarding second, third, and later marriages. But for this assessment process, it is essential to recognize that a theology of divorce and remarriage is typically reactive. It addresses how you will accept, minister to, and treat someone who has already gone through a divorce. It is a reactive theology. When it comes to marriage, churches need to become proactive. Rather than just establishing what we are going to do and how we are going to treat people after a marriage is already over, why don't we spend the same amount of time, energy, and reflection on God's Word to discern a theology of marriage? What's the difference between a theology of marriage, and a theology of divorce and remarriage? A theology of marriage is proactive. It is about seeing marriage as created and blessed by God, reflecting on what marriage is as participation in the kingdom of God, understanding marriage in relation to the church, and so much more.

In some fellowships, theology is handed down to local congregations from a hierarchy. A person or a group of people decide what their church's adherents should regard as authoritative and orthodox. Then those decisions are delivered to local leaders who relay it to the congregation, hopefully contextualizing it to their specific framework. In free church fellowships where there is no central headquarters, each congregation is autonomous and must discern its own theology. If a free church fellowship has a long-standing history and tradition, even though congregations are autonomous, there may be an inherited theology that is handed down and common to virtually all the congregations in that fellowship. By "inherited theology," I am referring to a theological viewpoint that is widespread, commonly held, and passed on from generation to generation with little or no change. Often, the theological viewpoint of an inherited theology becomes accepted based on tradition and comfortable familiarity rather than a careful, ongoing discernment of the contemporary culture through the lens of Scripture.

If your church's leadership does have a theology of marriage, regardless of whether it was handed down or was developed internally, take ample time to look at that theology. Study it. Seek to understand it. How did the people who articulated this theology come up with it? What was their context, and how is it the same or different from your context? How long ago did they articulate this theology? Decide if the theology needs to be readdressed. On what points do your team members perceive the theological statement the same? How do they see it differently?

If you church does not already have a theology of marriage, the following is a process for developing one. Please note that I am saying *a* process, not *the* process. There are many routes to establishing a well-thought out and well-articulated theology of marriage. You must choose the route that is best for your congregation.

The process described below uses group discernment. Why would you use group discernment rather than just letting a minister or church leader or someone trained in theology write up your marriage theology? For all the reasons we've talked about up till now. We all have different experiences of marriage. God works through different people in different ways. By using a group dynamic process you minimize many of the prejudices and the biases that can unintentionally creep into your marriage theology.

If you choose to use group discernment to generate a theology of marriage for your congregation, there are several important considerations. Group discernment is not throwing a bunch of people into a room and letting them all champion their opinion on a Scripture or topic. That is at best an opinion poll and at worst a pooling of ignorance.

First, you need to assemble your group. Look for people who have the spiritual gift of discernment. Usually, those with the gift of discernment are humble so they won't likely promote themselves. But, you can typically tell who shows wisdom, passion, appropriate restraint, and seeks to be a peacemaker without being a pushover. Like your marriage ministry team, you want to look for variety in your discernment group that adequately represents the demographics of your congregation. Some members of your marriage ministry team, if they are spiritually gifted with discernment, may be willing to serve in both capacities. It would be good to include at least a few of your church's main leaders. This will give more congregational authority to the process and assist in communicating to your full leadership the importance and vitality of what you are doing. In your discernment sessions, one person will need to take the lead to keep your group organized and on task, but everyone needs to participate. Remind the participants that each of them has been invited to be a part of the discernment group for a reason, and that each of them brings something unique to the table. Also, while advanced theology degrees are not necessary for participating, it is helpful to have people who have a good concept of and respect for strong theological discernment. Scripture, if taken out of context, can be made to say anything or support any cause. Make sure your discernment group participants have a healthy respect for the context and meaning of Scripture, and sound knowledge and practices on how to properly move from a passage's original context to your contemporary context.

Next, decide what aspect of marriage theology you are discerning. Are you looking for a general theology of marriage? Are you trying to articulate a theology that casts marriage as a special calling in the kingdom of God? Do you want to make a statement about the relationship of marriage to extended family? Are you only focusing on the covenant nature of marriage? Is your theology statement framed by marriage as service? There are multitudes of possible angles from which you can approach Christian marriage. There is a temptation to try and address it all, but limiting your focus will help you to say something much more meaningful to your congregational context. Remember, the theology you discern is the foundation for building your church's marriage ministry, but you don't have to develop an all-encompassing theological statement on your first outing using group discernment. Once you've gathered your discernment group and decided on your focus, select appropriate primary passages of Scripture for the group to study and work through in depth.

Before you begin your discernment sessions, make sure your discernment group knows to follow good group discernment practices. There are any numbers of works that describe discernment as a spiritual discipline and many of these would be helpful in establishing parameters for your group. My personal favorite is outlined in the eleventh chapter of Evan B. Howard's *The Brazos Introduction to Christian Spirituality* (Brazos Press, 2008). This work provides strong guidelines, reminders, and clarification for a discernment process, but is written in clear, easily understandable language. Whatever source you use, it is a good idea to post your general guidelines for the sessions so that your group is consistently reminded of what you are seeking to accomplish.

One major aspect for having a productive discernment task is to make sure your group understands the process of "push and push back." If the use of a discernment group is a new practice for you, your group participants might be tempted to fall into a normal weekly Bible class mode rather than a discernment group mode. Instead of an open discussion that allows for the freedom to agree and disagree, participants might attempt to try to come up with "the right answer." Rather than expressing theological reflection born out of their own life experiences, participants may at first remain silent, waiting to see if the person leading the sessions is fishing for a specific answer before they are willing speak out. The ability to disagree, and even do so forcefully and adamantly without fear of ridicule or ongoing animosity or distrust from others in the group, may not come immediately. Participants must be led to a place of comfortable dialogue with others in the group, even in disagreement, or real discernment will not take place.

Above all else, the discernment group must view their sessions together as a holy time, fully dedicated to God and trusting in God to lead them. And on a final note, don't rush the process. Sometimes discernment comes quickly, and sometimes it comes slowly. If your congregation is experiencing a high level of marital stress, you might be tempted to hurry things along. How many decisions have been reversed or regretted because the ongoing ramifications and consequences of those decisions weren't fully thought out? You cannot address every possible scenario or foresee every possible consequence, but don't rush the process and you will discern a much better theology of marriage from which to build.

The discernment process as it is described above is just a quick, bullet-point snapshot. There are many nuances and dimensions to group discernment. Regardless of how you get there, remember that your goal is to articulate a theology of marriage that is easily understood by the entire congregation, concise, contextually relevant, and fully born of Scripture.

Examples of marriage theology

Let's look at a couple of examples of what a marriage theology might look like. The first example is a general theology of marriage. Its goal was to establish a broad base from which the congregation could later further discern specific facets of the relationship between marriage and the church.

> ***What We Believe:***
>
> We believe that marriage was created by God (Gen. 1:26-2:25), was blessed by Christ (John 2:1-2; Matt. 19:4-6), and is empowered by the Holy Spirit (2 Cor. 3:2-3). We believe it is a covenant relationship between husband and wife, and God hates the breaking of covenant in divorce (Mal. 2:10-16). We believe marriage is intended to be a blessing to both husband and wife (Prov. 18:22). We believe that those who marry are to leave their parents' primary care to cleave to their spouses, and godly parents will facilitate rather than frustrate this God-ordained process (Gen. 2:24,

> Mark 10:6-9). We believe that husband and wife are to love each other in action as well as word (1 Cor. 13:4-8). A husband is to love his wife as Jesus loves the church, and a wife's love for her husband should be a witness of her love for God (Eph. 5:22-33). Wives and husbands are to submit to each other out of reverence for Christ (Eph. 5:21). We believe that God has not called everyone to marriage, and those who choose to remain single are equally important in the kingdom of God (Matt. 19:10-12).

As you look at this theology of marriage, there are several key points to note. These points are not necessarily things you must duplicate in your church's theology of marriage, but they are a good way of showing what was significant to the church that developed this theology at the time it was developed.

The theology states that God hates divorce, but it does not specify a first, second, third, or whatever number marriage—it simply says God hates divorce. The objective was to elevate and protect marriage, not be a theology statement on divorce and remarriage.

This theology uses the language of covenant and blessing. While those terms might need to be unpacked, they are powerful concepts that point back toward a spiritual foundation, basis, and origin for marriage.

Specific attention is given to the parents' role in this statement. It is ironic how often Christian parents can destroy their Christian child's Christian marriage to a Christian mate by not understanding the spiritual and physical implications of their role once their child marries.

This theology calls on couples to embrace love that is action and service-oriented and goes beyond shallow romanticism or self-serving motivations. Sacrificial love is the antithesis of the self-centered "is my mate meeting my needs" sentiment that permeates a worldly drive of marriage.

In crafting this theology statement, word choice was very intentional. Although the statement references Ephesians 5:21-33, in the statement the word "submit" is used when applied to the husband and wife together, but not when applied to the wife alone. In that sentence, a different way of articulating the same concept was chosen. Why? The English language is constantly changing. Words do not always mean what they used to mean. There's a reason children no longer sing "And we'll all be gay when Johnny comes marching home" in their music classes. Due to past abuses and misrepresentations, often in a religious context, the word "submit" can carry substantial baggage when applied only to the wife. This does not mean this church denies the validity of the biblical text or that they do not believe that wives should submit to their husbands. It simply means they felt there was another way to express the same concept in the modern vernacular that would make it clearer and more palatable to twenty-first century hearers.

And, although this is a marriage theology statement, this church felt it was still good and necessary to acknowledge the role of sacred singleness at their congregation. This move does not devalue the statement as a marriage theology statement. Rather, it helps put the statement into an overall framework for the church family.

The second theology of marriage is targeting a much more specific aspect of marriage than the general theology. This theological statement focuses on a husband and wife's role in the kingdom of God. Consider the following:

God's Call for Husbands and Wives at the Smyrna Church of Christ

> ***We believe*** that in the beginning God created humanity to be in relationship with Him. He created man and woman in His image (Gen. 1:26-27). Adam and Eve were created with a distinct purpose, to work together

in God's kingdom, participating with God by caring for creation and procreating (Gen. 1:28; 2:15). At creation, humanity's existence was fully focused on God. The physical life and the spiritual life were one together, and God was in their midst (Gen. 1-2).

We recognize that we fail to live out God's intent for husband and wife to participate with God. Sin entered the world breaking our spiritual and physical connection with God. With this came isolation, shame, fear, guilt, blame, loss of communication, and brokenness. Sin disrupts the marriage relationship and disrupts God's intention for husband and wife to partner together with Him to work in His kingdom (Gen. 3).

We rejoice that through the death and resurrection of our Lord Christ Jesus, God is calling husbands and wives back to a restored relationship with Him (2 Cor. 5:21). In Christ, God is calling us to participate in this reconciliation (2 Cor. 5:18-20). Through this participation, married couples are called to seek holiness, living lives of love, forgiveness, grace, healing, restoration, submission, and sacrificial living; with each other, within the church family, and toward the larger world of which we are a part. In Christ, husbands and wives participate together in reclaiming the relationship God established at creation, offer hope to others, and seek to reconcile the world back to God.

In marriage, husband and wife are "one flesh" (Gen. 2:23-24), working together in God's kingdom and sharing a common unity and a common purpose (Gen.

2:18). While the specifics of how a husband and wife particiate will differ from one couple to another, we believe a husband and wife's ongoing, joint participation is their intentional choice to please God and serve the cause of Christ (2 Cor. 5:15). We believe God is calling us as a church family to teach and live out this gospel of reconciliation as a path for husbands and wives to pursue together.

From the title, it is evident that this theological statement is intended for a specific congregation. While many of the things contained within it might translate to other congregations as well, that was not their intent in formulating this statement. It was intended to mean something specific to a specific group of Christians.

This marriage theology statement uses a four-paragraph movement to show original intent, current circumstances, God's resolution to our current predicament, and finally our response to God's call. In the third and fourth paragraphs, there is a very direct call for action from the couples at the specific congregation to which this is written.

However, the theology statement is careful not to outline specific actions since the number of ways a couple can participate in the kingdom of God and in the ministry of reconciliation is nearly limitless. Each couple is given the freedom to find their own path to respond, but the call is still a unified call to the whole congregation.

After you develop your theology of marriage, it is important that you have a plan for sharing the theology with the congregation. It doesn't matter how much time, prayer, and effort went into it. It doesn't matter how well-articulated it is. It doesn't matter how relevant it is to your congregation's situation. If it isn't shared with the congregation in a way that they can understand and incorporate it into the life of the community of faith, then it won't have the desired impact.

The first step is to always bring your theology into a written form. There are some key reasons for this. First, when something is written down, it is far more concrete than if it is just an idea, no matter how good an idea, that is just floating around. Second, if something has been a part of your church culture for an extended period of time, it becomes ingrained in who you are and you forget that new faces haven't lived your church experience. When your marriage theology is written down, you have a definitive touchpoint to share with them. Third, a written form serves as a definitive reference point for the congregation when discussing the theology and expanding upon it. Although your discernment group may initially be in agreement on your congregation's theology of marriage, if there isn't something written down to remind them and others of what they discerned, it becomes easy to forget and multiple interpretations can emerge as discernment group members' recollections fade or as others who were not a part of the discernment group misinterpret or misunderstand what is shared with them.

When you put it into written form, carefully consider the words you use. Remember, by the time you get to this point your discernment group has been living and breathing this theology for a long, long time. How would someone read the marriage theology statement who did not study the primary passages as in depth as you did? Does your statement communicate your theology of marriage in a way that is easily understood by the entire congregation, concise, contextually relevant, and fully born of Scripture?

Finally, you have to decide how you plan to communicate your theology of marriage to the congregation. If it is not communicated to the congregation, no matter how good your intentions in discerning the theology, you have wasted your time. There are so many ways that you can share your theology of marriage with your church family. Some possibilities include a sermon or series of sermons, through bulletin articles, a special class or congregational meeting, or maybe in a brochure or other special publication specifically dedicated to marriage. Whatever method you choose, unless your members are aware, they cannot act upon that theology to change the marriage culture within the congregation.

Constant repetition is the most powerful way to ingrain something into a given culture or context. Moses admonished the Israelites to constantly replay their story. They were to remind themselves and remind their children who they were as God's chosen people by consistently repeating those identifying marks (Deuteronomy 6:1-11, et al.). After you initially communicate your marriage theology to the congregation, have a plan in place to keep that theology in front of the church family. If you present it once, no matter how great the fanfare surrounding the presentation, it will quickly be forgotten if the church family is not periodically reminded—not just of the words of the theology statement, but also the significance of a strong marriage theology for the overall health of the congregation. How you choose to do that will vary from church to church. One congregation printed huge banners with their marriage theology and hung them in the sanctuary. As people entered and left each week this served as a constant visual reminder, not just of the theology itself, but of its importance to the church family.

Your marriage theology has the potential to change the teachings and practices of your congregation for generations to come. However, the theological statement produced should be reevaluated periodically. The spiritual, physical, contextual, and cultural situations that caused you to establish your marriage theology statement to begin with are ever changing. As the contemporary culture and the church culture continue to change, the worst possible response to the need that led to discerning a marriage theology would be to allow the theology statement produced to become an inherited theology that may no longer be relevant to the makeup of your congregation in the future.

Finding the heart of your marriage ministry

The primary calling of all Christians is to love God and love one's neighbor (Matthew 22:34-40). Love for one's neighbor is the physical manifestation of their love for God. Since God does not live among us in a corporeal form or otherwise engage us in a physical manner, it is easy to profess love for God. Yet our relationship with God is reflected by our interaction with our fellow humanity. As the image bearer of God, the way we interact with others who are also made in God's image reveals how fully conformed to the likeness of God we are becoming. "Whoever claims to love God yet hates a brother or sister is a liar. For whoever does not love their brother and sister, whom they have seen, cannot love God, whom they have not seen" (1 John 4:20).

Without a doubt, your spouse is your closest, most intimate neighbor. Regardless of whether a person is initially compelled to marriage for carnal reasons, spiritual reasons, or some combination of the two, the call of marriage is to love God as evidenced by love for his or her spouse. Although the pursuit of love for God is the primary goal, it is inseparable from the pursuit of loving your mate.

Within the context of marriage, we must understand the concept of "one flesh" as more than a platitude or a reference only to the sexual nature of humanity. We must see one flesh as the communal calling of marriage in light of God's call to love him and love your neighbor. Marriage is an entirely unique participation in the divine mystery of a holistic oneness between man, woman, and God that reflects Christ's relationship with the church (Ephesians 5:21-33). In marriage, couples find a joint purpose in God that transcends the couple's sharing of a home and a bed. Marriage becomes the vessel in which couples grow in holiness together while participating in reconciling creation back to God through their life in Christ. It is the purposeful reorientation of life toward discipleship as it is specifically expressed in your relationship with your mate. It is a visible, outward manifestation of covenant living, commitment, intimacy, grace, forgiveness, and love. It is the means by which a husband and wife truly become "salt and light" to the world around them.

As you complete the third and final stage of listening, listen to the theological voice of marriage that is present at your congregation. Even if your church is not saying anything in regard to a theology of marriage, the silence is saying something. If you believe Christian marriage is something uniquely different from the world's view of marriage, it all begins with your congregation's theology of marriage. Your theology of marriage truly is the heart of what your marriage ministry is and what it will become. What does the beating heart of your marriage ministry pump throughout the body of believers at your congregation?

Chapter 7

Phase 4: Sorting It All Out

Have you ever worked on one of those massive jigsaw puzzles with a group of friends? You know the kind I'm talking about. You see the really cool picture on the box, and you are convinced you can put that picture together. So, you go home, open the box and dump the puzzle pieces out on the kitchen table. Then, as you and your friends quickly flip over piece after piece after piece, you notice so many of the pieces are hard to distinguish. Those little bits of image don't look anything like the picture on the box. And the colors, you didn't realize how many blue pieces there were, or yellow, or green. As everyone joins in to help you with the puzzle, you disagree over which way a piece goes, or if that piece is a part of a leg or a part of a building in the background. But eventually, with enough time and patience and sharing of pieces, the image begins to become clear. First, a border into which everything else must fit is pieced together. Then small sections that neatly fit together. Eventually the smaller sections are positioned together to make even larger portions become clear. Finally, the last piece is put in place. Although each individual piece is there, you have something wholly different from the thousand individual pieces with which you started out.

From the beginning of this assessment process to this point has been a long journey. To get to here, you have spent weeks, months, or maybe even a year or more listening, observing, collecting information, separating perception from reality, and generally seeing what the true condition and belief about marriage in your congregation is. Also, you have hopefully at least begun the process of finding a strong theological voice of marriage for your congregation. Now, what do you do with all that information?

It's time for the team to pull it all together, to take the individual pieces they have collected, and to form one shared image of marriage with your congregation. This is a time of personal and group reflection, as you make sense of everything you've done up to this point. The entire team needs to come together for as many meetings as it takes to wade through what everyone has discovered. As you work your way through this stage of the process, you will see many similarities and many differences. Information that you believe reveals one thing may seem to say something totally different to another team member. But as you persevere in discerning together, the pieces will begin to fit. Different pieces will make up different parts of the image, but eventually, it will all form one cohesive image. Once the image is clear, the team will share with the church's leadership what they've discovered, and, based on the reality of the church's marriage situation, begin to map out a plan for the future. The end result of this stage of the assessment process should be a consolidated written report that you will present to the leadership of your congregation.

Some guiding thoughts and questions for making sense of it all

Just as with first three stages (listening to the whispers in the hallways, hearing your statistical analysis, and paying attention to the formal voice of marriage your congregation projects) there are some guiding thoughts and questions that will help you put the puzzle pieces together. Although these thoughts and questions are presented somewhat systematically here, the information garnered will overlap and flow back and forth from question to question throughout your team's conversations.

In reviewing your findings over the last several weeks, what would you assess to be the general climate of marriage at your church?

Start with the big picture. Let each marriage ministry team member share his or her general sense of marriage at your church.

Is your church proactive or reactive (or inactive) in regard to marriage? Explain your answer.

Because we do place a high value on godly, healthy, Christian marriages, most churches are at least trying to do something (otherwise you wouldn't be engaging in this assessment process to begin with). But what does each team member see as strengths and weaknesses to your current response to the relationship between marriages and your church culture?

How do your findings compare to the rest of the team's findings?

As the old Christmas carol says, "Do you hear what I hear?" Where are your observations similar? Where are they different? You are still listening, but now you are listening to see what the other team members heard.

To what do you attribute differing viewpoints within the team?

What can affect a team member's perspective? Anything from age, to the length of time married, to knowledge of the congregation and its history, to personal background, to generational biases can affect someone's perspective. What an older team member sees as harmless kidding, a younger team member may see as hurtful criticism. If you grew up in a hostile home where mom and dad argued constantly, you might be more sensitive to displays of anger than someone who grew up in a more peaceful setting. What someone in their 20s sees as a critical, marriage-threatening problem, someone in their 70s realizes is just a bump on the journey that is marriage. On and on the list can go of potential differences team members must sort through.

In your conversations with team members, it is necessary to remember the concept of push and push back as described in the last chapter. Team members need to be able to present and defend their perceptions without fear of ridicule or animosity. Every voice is important to assembling an overall picture. If any piece is missing, the puzzle is not complete.

Is your view of the state of marriage at your church the same as it was before you began this process?

Share specific observations, both negative and positive, with the group that have surprised you as you have engaged in this discovery process. Where has your congregation really shined brightly? Where have you seen or heard things that have shocked you?

As your marriage ministry team engages in these conversations, undoubtedly you will discuss particular things you have seen and heard specific individuals say or do. Throughout these conversations you will do well to remind your team members of the importance of a strict confidentiality. Because marriage is about real human relationships, because we exhibit the good, the bad, and the ugly, even (and sometimes most often) with those we love most, you might hear things about specific couples or individuals that will cause you to reassess your current views. Your team members must be able to process that information and maintain the necessary conduct to insure the trust of your membership.

Now what?

You've had your meetings. You have put together the pieces and your team now has a unified consensus of marriage in your congregation. What do you do with this information?

The next step is to bring this information to your church's leadership. Even if you have church leaders as a part of your marriage ministry team, you need to schedule a meeting with the full leadership. In preparation for that meeting, put together a written report about the state of marriage at your congregation. Although one person from your marriage ministry team may be tasked with bringing your findings into a written form, the entire team should be given time to proofread and offer corrections or amendments to the report. This report does not need to be "Doug thinks this, Suzie thinks this, Charlie thinks this…" It needs to be the consensus of the group that was discerned as described above. Although you may cite specific individual team member's insights, this is not a comparison and contrast of different viewpoints among team members.

Even if you plan to give an oral report, you also need the written report to allow your leadership to have something definitive in hand to take with them from the meeting. And, it would be beneficial if you know exactly what your leadership plans to do with the information you bring back to them. If the report is to be kept only as an internal document it might be presented one way, but if the report is to be shared with the congregation, it might be presented another way. Regardless of how the information is to be utilized, but especially if it is to be shared beyond your marriage ministry team and your church leaders, you must be certain that names are not named and there are not any instances of information, examples, or anecdotes that could be linked back to a specific individual or couple. Without confidentiality, there will be no trust.

After you've delivered your findings to your church's leadership, schedule a time to meet with them again to discuss proactive means of enhancing (or possibly completely changing) the fabric of marriage in your congregation. Why plan a second meeting with your leadership after you have reported your findings to them? First, it will give them time to digest what you have discovered. The months of listening your team engaged in cannot be distilled into a one- or two-hour long meeting. If you had misconceptions, it is likely your church leaders have the same misconceptions. They will be just as surprised, shocked, and disoriented by what you've heard and observed as you were. They may have questions beyond what they think to ask in the initial meeting. They may request follow-up meetings to clarify things in your report. Allow them time to reorient themselves to the new reality.

And second, while they are digesting and processing your report, it will give your marriage ministry team time to meet and begin to brainstorm on proactive marriage ministry initiatives. This is the point that too many churches want to jump to without assessing their true situation and establishing their theological foundation first. In many ways, the initiation phase, which is detailed in the next chapter, will be the most challenging phase yet. But, Lord willing, it will also be the most rewarding.

Chapter 8

Phase 5: Ready, Set, Action!

In the last chapter, I used the analogy of a puzzle for putting together the pieces you've collected up to this point. Lord willing, when you look at that image of that pieced-together puzzle, you will see not only a reflection of the state of marriage at your congregation, but also a map. When you look at the state of marriage in your church, what does it tell you about where you need to go next?

If you came to this point expecting to be given a step-by-step plan for initiating a marriage ministry, you will be disappointed. As I said from the outset, it is not my purpose to tell you what your marriage ministry should look like. That needs to be dictated by your own congregation, your time and place, and the things you discovered up to this point. In this chapter, I will help you make sense of your context as best I can, but ultimately, it's up to your own community of faith to move forward in making a culture of healthy marriages a part of the fabric of who you are as a congregation of God's people.

Diving into this stage of the process will be a very exciting time as you begin to postulate ways your months of work can bear fruit. After a long time of passive listening, it's time for active involvement! When you come to the point of beginning various initiatives in your marriage ministry, remember two things. First, change is always a challenge. Depending on the extent that change is needed, the actions you propose for couples at your church can range from mildly uncomfortable to downright scary. Again, it is easy to forget that the majority of your congregation has not been immersed in this process like your team has. If change is needed, change must come, but change always encounters resistance. There are some good guides for helping churches navigate change. Peter L. Steinke's *Congregational Leadership in Anxious Times* (The Alban Institute, 2006) is a very helpful read. Second, remember that the larger the ship is, the slower it will turn. The larger your congregation is or the deeper its history and tradition, the longer it will take to initiate wide-scale change. Change can be made, but it might have to happen incrementally rather than as a one hundred eighty degree turn on a dime. I don't offer these cautions to deter you from doing what needs to be done, but to remind you that it took time for your congregation to get to its current state of marriage, and it will take time to move it somewhere better.

And with that being said, it is time to consider the physical realities of this spiritual ministry. All of your work up to this point was for naught if you don't actually do something with it to better the marriages within your congregation. Just as faith without works is dead, so too is a congregation's marriage ministry if they know what ought to be done, but don't actually do it. Below are things your marriage ministry team will want to consider as you put flesh on the bones of your marriage ministry. First, let's start with overarching general considerations that impact everything that flows out of this ministry.

Have you prayed throughout this process?

Hopefully, prayer has been an integral part of every single step of this process from the beginning till now. Now is not the time to lay prayer aside. Pray even more adamantly now, because as necessary as everything up to this point has been, at this point you are going to be initiating things that will have a direct, physical impact on marriages in your church. No matter how good something looks on paper, how well you think you understand something, or how carefully you have planned, when you begin intersecting with real lives you're going to need Divine guidance.

Are you willing to let God lead you rather than do what you want to do and ask God to bless it?

So many times, well-intentioned church folks get it backwards. How often have you heard someone pray "Lord, bless the decision we made." Obviously, we do have to make decisions, and yes, we do want God to bless those decisions. But do you make plans and then try to retrofit God into your plans, or, do you listen attentively to God's leading before you commit yourselves to a course of action? And, do you continue to pray and listen as you proceed, knowing that sometimes God makes adjustments to the path as we move forward? "Unless the LORD builds the house, the builders labor in vain. Unless the LORD watches over the city, the guards stand watch in vain" (Psalm 127:1).

Are you thinking "program" or "process"? Are you thinking "immediate results" or "long-term ministry"?

If you miss it on this you have missed the entire point of this book. The goal of this assessment process is to establish identity. How does Christian marriage fit into the church's identity? Programs are a means of communicating a church's identity, but don't confuse the program with its purpose. And while I do pray that you do get quick results for healthier marriages, remember, the race is not always to the swift, but also to those who can keep running. What will Christian marriage at your congregation mean to the next generation and the next?

Are the ideas you are considering equally applicable to couples in this congregation, regardless of the socio-economic status, age, ethnicity, or other distinctions?

While every ministry initiative doesn't have to apply to every couple, every time, are you taking into account the reality of the couples you are serving? You might plan the most innovative, exciting, spirit-filled couples' getaway ever, but if the cost winds up being five hundred dollars per couple and your congregation is a mostly blue collar rural community in a depressed economic time, then your efforts were in vain. How can you best integrate your spiritual family in a way that won't add more stress to their lives?

How willing is the leadership of the church to fully support the initiatives you propose?

Everything you've done up to this point has been crucial to understanding where you want to go, but it has also been passive, still existing primarily in the world of research, assumption, and belief. At the beginning of the process, I stated that your leadership must be fully on board. At the beginning of the process, they did not yet know what you would find as it was detailed in the report on the state of marriage in your congregation that you presented to them, so endorsing this process was more of an academic support. The rock has not yet been thrown into the still waters, and when it is, the leaders are the ones who will have to deal with the ripples. Now is the time for action, and your leadership is being called upon to show courage as they consider your proposed initiatives. Pray adamantly with them and for them as you prepare to move forward from a reactive culture to a proactive culture.

How willing is your team to submit to your leadership's wisdom and guidance in refining or (possibly) eliminating things you feel strongly about?

Your leadership is well aware that change can bring about resistance and potential problems, and as congregational leaders, they are ultimately responsible for shepherding that congregation of believers. After all of your work, time, and effort, one of the most discouraging things to hear is "no," or "not like that." But when that happens, perhaps the test is not upon your leadership's courage, but upon your trust and faith.

Often, the leadership of a congregation is aware of things to which the general membership is oblivious. When you propose a ministry, your leaders may know of factors that would adversely affect that ministry, but due to confidentiality they are not at liberty to discuss those factors with your team. Make your best case for what you believe to be the right thing to do, but regardless of whether you hear the answer you want or not, you must trust that it is God's church and he loves it and will take care of it. Remember, you are working as a team for the good of the congregation, not for individual credit or accolades.

Is everything you are doing guided by your congregation's theology of marriage? How do you move toward that stated theology becoming the predominant voice of marriage in your church?

We have already discussed the importance of getting your theology of marriage before the congregation, but putting theology into action is always a more daunting task than just mentally or vocally affirming something. Every initiative must reconnect your congregation in some way to your church's theology of marriage. If it doesn't, you are stepping off of the foundation for your marriage ministry and walking on the shifting sands of a reactive church culture.

As you work through a ministry initiative, specific considerations will quickly begin to emerge. Don't gloss over the general considerations above, but also be prepared to wrestle with the questions that will have a more direct impact as you plan specific initiatives. The information below will help you navigate the more detailed considerations.

Target:
Is there a specific segment of your congregation that you need to address first?

Go back to your research to see where best to concentrate resources. Is a ministry initiative hitting your target audience or is it geared toward a different demographic? After your beginning initiatives, how will you expand your marriage ministry to be comprehensive?

Timetable:
Do you have a definitive time line for beginning a ministry initiative?

Again, depending on how critical marriages in your congregation were prior to beginning this assessment and how critical they are now, there might be a pressing urgency. But remember, you can't do everything at once. If a full-scale marriage ministry is something new to your congregation, concentrate on doing a few things well and grow from there.

Sustainability:
Is an idea maintainable?

Do you have the necessary resources for the ministry idea you are proposing? What will it cost in financial resources? Human resources? Is this something that couples will engage in with great enthusiasm initially, but quickly become burned out? How willing are others to pick up this ministry idea over time?

Just because an idea is a really great idea, should every idea be a permanent fixture? When do you let something go in favor of another idea or another format? And, are you prepared to let "your baby" go in favor of something more relevant at a later time? The last thing you want to do is have your marriage ministry slip into a "because that's the way we've always done it" mode.

What initiatives do become ongoing parts of the congregational identity?

This might be anything from pre-marital counseling to regulations regarding the use of your building for weddings to professional counseling services. Certain things do need to be permanent fixtures. The way those things are presented or utilized may need to change over time, but what are the things that make definitive statements about you as a church and your belief about Christian marriage?

Are you growing your marriage ministry plans as marriages grow and the marriage makeup of your congregation changes?

The 20s and 30s class doesn't stay the 20s and 30s class forever. Before long, they are the 30s and 40s class, and the things they once did are no longer possible. The pre-children, spontaneous couples' camping trip getaway is now sidelined by Saturday soccer games, and the couples-only Thursday night volleyball has given way to arthritis pain.

How well do your ministry initiatives meet the *current* needs of couples? When ministry initiatives do evolve over time to meet the needs of an aging group of couples, are you remembering to do things to minister to younger couples coming into the congregation, addressing the issues and trials specific to their marriages?

How adaptable is a specific marriage ministry idea?

The life or death of a ministry initiative may lie in its adaptability. How willing are you to change an idea you have proposed? Rigidity can be the death of a good idea that could greatly benefit couples in your congregation. Sometimes the changes are minor, and sometimes an idea has to go through a major overhaul. Sometimes the target demographic has to be reassigned, and sometimes the focus has to be realigned. Even the best conceived, most well-thought-out ministry ideas will have to be changed from time to time.

Keeping it fresh

There's nothing better than a fresh, hot Krispy Kreme donut, when the neon "hot" sign is lit up and you watch the freshly baked delicacy move down the conveyer through the waterfall of glaze. They just simply melt in your mouth! At our house, a dozen fresh Krispy Kremes don't last long. If we buy them at night, they will generally be gone by breakfast the next morning. If a few do remain till morning, they are still good, but nowhere near as good as they were on the ride home from the donut shop, when you could still feel the warm box on your lap. Once in a blue moon, a donut or two will be left for two days. Even more rarely, we'll lay the box aside and a donut may linger for several days. Eventually, if we forget about them for too long, that once hot, fresh treat is hard, stale and only fit for the trash can.

The longer a ministry is in full swing, the greater the possibility it can grow stale and stagnate. But if healthy Christian marriages are a priority, you don't want to stop trying. You don't want to lose momentum. You especially don't want to compromise on your theological impetus or on your place as a part of the DNA of who you are as a congregation. So what do you do to remain fresh and relevant to your congregation?

Sometimes remaining fresh is as simple as being aware and recognizing changes that are occurring in the church and secular cultures around you. Consider simple questions like: Are you using varying formats or are things always done in the same way? Do you use guest speakers with expertise in marriage or have you limited couples in your congregation to just one or two voices on marriage? Are you utilizing different learning formats? An older couple's method for taking in information may be radically different than a younger couple's. Are you using media resources and technology to its fullest potential? Well-chosen clips from movies or television shows can be some of the most powerful teaching tools out there. Are you consistently looking at different curriculums to see what is available? There are many good curriculums, but for every good resource on marriage there are a dozen poor resources. And, what's good for one congregation may not be good for another, so you have to evaluate curriculum based on your own context. New books and material relative to Christian marriage are coming out all the time, so staying on top of the best material is an ongoing process.

In addition to curriculum and books, are you aware of the tools that are available to help evaluate couples' situations and needs? There are major assessment instruments like PREPARE/ENRICH, but there are also dozens of other surveys and assessments on a smaller scale that do not require formal training to administer and interpret. Sometimes those lesser-known tools can provide a wealth of information about the state of marriage in the congregation. At my home congregation, using a simple assessment tool, we were able to determine a disturbing trend in which several husbands and wives had sharply differing views of the state of their marriage. The assessment revealed that in about one in ten cases of the couples surveyed, one spouse believed the marriage to be strong or stable while the other spouse believed it to be strained or in severe jeopardy. By utilizing this assessment as we did, we were able to help these couples recognize the difference in their perceptions of their relationships and begin the process of restoring a healthy relationship. Had we not made the effort to keep abreast of current tools, we might have missed the opportunity to help these couples. Keeping fresh benefits your ministry thus benefiting your congregation.

Using what you've already got

At the end of the month, as our grocery budget begins to grow thin, Lisa looks in the pantry and freezer and sees the odds and ends items that are not the quick, easy favorites. She can't make another trip to the grocery just yet, and she doesn't want to waste what we have, but she's not exactly sure how to make the available ingredients into a meal we'll all enjoy? So what does she do? Thankfully, Lisa is aware of a few websites where you can type in the ingredients you have on hand, and it will generate a plethora of recipes that use what you already have; often things you might have never thought of before. The result is a great meal that utilizes what we already have, doesn't require additional shopping, and helps control expenses.

As you and your marriage ministry team brainstorm on marriage ministry initiatives, don't forget to use what you already have. The last thing many churches need is another full-scale, heavily-programmed ministry that demands time, volunteers, its own budget lines, and other precious resources. One of the best first steps you can take in beginning or improving your congregation's marriage ministry is to evaluate the ministries you already have in place and discern how you can incorporate healthy marriages into those already existing ministries. We often forget that it can be more beneficial for the congregation to at least begin by working within the framework of existing ministries. If you've ever been in an unfamiliar city with everyone around you speaking a different language, you know how relieved you feel when you see a familiar face or hear someone you can understand. By using existing ministries, you are still achieving your goal of facilitating kingdom-focused marriages, but you are couching it in familiar terrain.

Review each ministry for current and potential avenues for husbands and wives to participate together. The purpose is not to take over viable ministries led by capable people in order to force a ministry to fit into a preconceived mold for marriage ministry, but rather as a means of helping ministry leaders recognize and expand on new venues of participation in their respective ministries. You shouldn't expect every ministry will provide practical means for husbands and wives to have joint participation but, the majority of ministries at many churches have never considered the paths available for a couple's joint participation.

For example, a church's senior citizens ministry provides an ideal place for older couples to help mentor younger couples. In children's and youth classes, husbands and wives can teach together, chaperone events together, and find multiple ways to show marriage is about joint participation in God's kingdom. Most missions ministries offer various ways for couples to actively take part in spreading the gospel together. A small groups ministry can give more intimate settings for couples to encourage each other to live out the call of your church's marriage theology. In small groups, couples can also share ideas for non-church driven ways for husbands and wives to be active in the kingdom together. Even men's and women's ministries can be reviewed for ways to facilitate healthy marriages. Everything from complementary classes that focus on husbands' and wives' roles in actively participating together in the kingdom of God to things each spouse can do to honor his or her mate are possibilities. Why not have a husband and wife visitation team rather than making visitation strictly a men's ministry or women's ministry activity? What other types of service opportunities does your congregation offer? How much tweaking would it take to make it conducive to spouses working together? These are just a few examples of the potential changes that could occur within already established ministries.

Remember, the goal of your marriage ministry is not a hostile takeover of the church's other ministries. It is the holistic integration of healthy, proactive, kingdom-focused marriages into every aspect of your congregation's life.

Flash in the pan or lasting ministry

My church puts on a fantastic summer Bible camp. I have been a part of summer Bible camps for several decades, and we have refined the process to make it a spectacular event. The core of our camp is always a strong spiritual focus. That focus is accentuated by a great family feel and lots and lots of cool games and activities. Summer Bible camp is indeed a very special time and place each year. There is no doubt in my mind that during that week, we are in the presence of God, seeing him work in powerful ways in the lives of children, teens, and adults. I feel so strongly about camp that each year when it is over, I feel an emptiness within. It is hard to describe, but it is almost a melancholy feeling as I come down from a mountain-top experience that I have been blessed to help plan and carry out.

If that's all there was to camp, it would be a great event, but not much more. And great events have their place in the life of a church. But summer Bible camp is so much more because even though the event ends, we continue to follow up on the relationships developed at camp each year. It's not just new friendships growing, but it is also existing relationships achieving deeper levels of spiritual intimacy, accountability, and forward momentum for the kingdom of God. Summer Bible camp is the event, but it is only the beginning point of ministry that continues throughout the year.

As you plan your marriage ministry initiatives, there is a real temptation to turn your marriage enrichment initiatives into events. And, as I said, events can be good and do have their place in the life of a church. It's great when people can get excited over a couples retreat, or a seminar, or a class on healthy marriage. I wish more couples would find indescribable joy in the announcement of a mentoring program or in finding their place for joint participation in the kingdom of God through a marriage small group. But if the event is all there is, your marriage ministry team will have a real problem.

The problem with an "events" mentality is that it produces a "bigger and better" conundrum. Everything you do has to be better than the last thing you did: more hype, better attendance, more initial excitement. But is your goal the event itself, or the lasting change that emanates from your efforts? An "events" mentality causes burn-out with your team and eventual stagnation because it is a cycle that cannot be indefinitely perpetuated. Should your marriage ministry contain exciting events? Of course, but pray and plan beyond the event itself. If you don't, your marriage ministry will be a blip on the radar screen of the history of your congregation; just a lot of cool things people remember fondly, but with no real life-changing, church-culture-changing power.

Be prepared for failure

Never forget, the other side is at work too. As hard as you and your team are working to improve marriages in your congregation, the devil is working just as hard to destroy marriages in your congregation. Sometimes the attacks will be blatant and outright. Sometimes the attacks will be subtle. The devil may strike from outside your congregation through cultural and community changes. Other times, he may strike from within your congregation through church members who constantly complain or deliberately sabotage your efforts. Sometimes the attacks may come through your own pride or through a failure to discern the times and the needs of marriages within the congregation.

And sometimes failure might not be the devil at work. Sometimes your failure might be the voice of God. How can God be behind our failure in fostering stronger, healthier, more spiritually based marriages? Timing is everything. Sometimes, a good idea may have just come at the wrong time. Moses was a great leader. He had a strong sense of justice and he wanted to do what was right. So, when Moses stepped up and took care of an Egyptian taskmaster beating a Hebrew slave, it seemed like what God would have wanted. Because Moses was working on his own timetable and under his own assumptions and authority, he wound up herding sheep in the desert for the next forty years. Right person, right spirit, wrong time. But God eventually did use Moses. And because it was on God's timetable and by God's design, God used Moses in ways far beyond what Moses could have ever imagined as a forty-year-old defending a Hebrew slave.

Brainstorming with your marriage ministry team and with your leadership on marriage ministry initiatives is an exciting time. When things begin to happen, when you can really see powerful, positive changes happening within your congregation, be thankful that God is working through you to his glory and the good of his kingdom. But when failure comes, how will your marriage ministry respond? You can either let failure define you or refine you. Nobody likes to fail, but failure is a time to reaffirm your commitment to listening to the voice of God and resisting the devil so that he will flee from his attacks on marriages in your congregation.

Chapter 9

Keeping It Alive

If you have been a part of a church for any length of time, you have probably seen more than one ministry take off with great excitement and pomp, only to have it become a distant memory six months later. As with any endeavor like this, the immediate question becomes, "How do we keep it alive?" You have done all this work—research, planning, praying—you have invested precious time and resources—and now the ministry has launched. By all accounts, it is up and running, hopefully well-received, and you are beginning to see positive changes within your congregation. So now what? How do you not become just another failed ministry attempt?

For something to remain in the collective conscience of a congregation, it often takes a person or group of people with a passion for that ministry to keep it at the forefront. Otherwise it will quickly be moved to the back burner. It certainly takes an ongoing recognition of spiritual necessity and importance from the leadership of your congregation.

It is human nature to ignore the really important in favor of the really urgent. You must decide if the marriages in your congregation are *always* important, or only when failure of marriages makes the situation really urgent. I believe the state of Christian marriage at most churches has been really urgent for some time. If you always make Christian marriage really important, you will be better equipped to proactively deal with marriage problems when the really urgent sounds its alarm.

The good news is, if you have done everything up to this point to lay a strong, biblically-focused, contextually-relevant foundation it will be easier to maintain a healthy, ongoing, proactive marriage ministry than it would be to build or rebuild one from scratch. The key is in remembering to keep focusing on the basic principles that you began building upon. Continue to listen to the voices of marriage in your congregation. By this point, the predominant voice of marriage should be your congregation's theology of marriage. If it currently isn't the predominant voice, hopefully you have positioned it to eventually become that main voice. In chapter six, I already outlined some ways to keep your theology of marriage in front of the congregation, but be sure to keep it in front of your marriage ministry team as well. If the theology of marriage stops being the predominant voice your marriage ministry team listens to, it will quickly stop being your congregation's predominant voice. Also, remember to periodically review your marriage theology statement to make sure it is remaining biblically-based and contextually-pertinent. Don't allow neglect to cause your primary voice to become irrelevant to your congregation, either by not calling couples to a higher standard or by not connecting to the reality of their lives.

Don't go on cruise control

For many years, my family has traveled from middle Tennessee to Hilton Head Island, South Carolina for vacation. We are always excited to go on vacation, and for the most part the six-hundred-mile drive has many interesting sights that we look forward to seeing each year. The only part of the drive that we dread is the stretch from

Macon, Georgia to Savannah, Georgia on Interstate 16. It's a good road. It's smooth and uneventful. Traffic is exceptionally light. The problem is it is as boring as can be. For three hours, the landscape looks the same; nothing but large fields and an occasional country road. The exits are few and far between, and if you get off at an exit, you still have to drive miles to find a gas station or somewhere to eat. It is just plain boring. Because the drive is relatively effortless and because there are never any real surprises, it is incredibly easy to set the minivan on cruise control and basically shut off any thinking about driving except for the most basic functions.

Don't let your marriage ministry go on cruise control. When things are going nicely, when the atmosphere is positive, when the programs are running well, and when there are no real surprises on the horizon, it is easy to sit back and let the ministry run itself. The problem is, when you let the ministry run itself and you let the programs take over, well, that's when an eighteen wheeler suddenly decides to changes lanes right in front of you, and you have no choice but to react. And, a knee-jerk reaction usually causes anxiety and fosters an atmosphere of reactivity rather than proactivity.

Don't become a program, become part of the congregational identity. Programs come and go, but the identity of the congregation abides. Make sure your marriage ministry is a place of authenticity, hope, and healing. Teach your church to practice their Christianity first and foremost at home with their spouse. Help make "till death do we part" once again be seen as a wonderful blessing rather than a dreaded life-sentence!

Continue also to listen to the informal and formal voices of marriage in your congregation. While it is no longer the methodical, organized listening outlined in phase one and three of the assessment process, you and your marriage ministry team still need to be attentive to the spirit and law of marriage that is projected by your congregation. Small course corrections are always easier to manage than huge turnabouts. If you become aware of things that alarm you or you feel are counter to your congregation's theology of marriage and your leadership's desire for marriage at your church, then alert your leadership to what you are hearing. Regular ongoing conversations between the marriage ministry team and your church's leadership will help keep everyone on the same page about what you are hearing and how you need to respond to those voices.

Make sure new adherents are aware of your congregation's position on marriage. If it is not important to your leadership it won't be important to new members. Have a definitive plan in place with whomever interviews or acknowledges or orients new members at your church. Letting new members know about your church's position on Christian marriage does not have to be an overbearing hard sell, but it also shouldn't be an "oh, and by the way, there's this too" afterthought. Be sure to train the new member orientation team on how to contextualize your church's marriage theology to the new member's situation. If she is divorced, she needs to know why the marriage theology is still important to her. If he is single, he still needs to understand how healthy marriages in the congregation impact his walk with Christ.

Just as it is important to listen to the informal and formal voices of marriage on an ongoing basis, it is also critical to continually recognize the marriage landscape of your congregation. Once you do the initial work of gathering the info, it becomes a much easier process to keep it updated. Just as it was the first time you mapped out the landscape of your congregation, this information will be a constant reference for understanding where you need to concentrate resources and provide ministry and counseling. Consistently updated information is also a safeguard against letting time slip up on you and failing to recognize the changing needs of couples as they grow older and go through various stages of life.

An accurate picture of the marriage landscape can also give you a means for helping marriages through crises. As you chart statistical information, you can also create a database of couples who can help in specific events. Consider the number of things that can rock a marriage

- Miscarriage/Death of a child
- An affair
- Loss of a job
- Bankruptcy
- Depression
- Having to become the caregiver for an aging/dying parent
- Sudden or significant changes in health
- Abuse
- Addiction
- Parenting crises

The list could go on and on. No matter what the circumstance, chances are there is another couple in your congregation who has walked the road ahead of the couple currently embroiled in the situation. Those couples who have real-life experience, who have come through the valley and come out the other side stronger in their faith and in their commitment to God and to each other, can typically provide the most comfort and the most hope. At my congregation, if a couple loses a child to a miscarriage, I know another couple to direct them to for guidance and comfort. If a couple loses a teenage child, we have someone who can help. If money problems are wrecking a relationship, there is another couple that can offer hope.

Obviously, not everyone is willing or is well-suited to give counsel or comfort to others. But for those who are, it is a powerful ministry to the couples in need of help and for the couples providing help.

And often, those couples who are willing to help others might not be the first to volunteer. Sometimes you might need to help them recognize the power of their own story as a part of God's work in bringing healing and reconciliation to other couples. A consistently updated landscape of marriage for your congregation will allow you to keep your eyes open to ways the Lord can work through your church's couples to strengthen marriages for the Kingdom of God.

Chapter 10

Difficult Conversations

The Central Church downtown was facing a crisis. The congregation has a one-hundred-year history of being a stronghold for truth and compassion. Members were active during the Great Depression era, serving food and providing what encouragement they could to those who were out of work and hurting. Even as the city grew up around them, they continued to boldly preach the gospel while opening up their building as a shelter for the homeless. They were keenly aware of the grip the devil had on those outside of their congregation, but now they were facing a crisis from within.

Chad and his family had been members of the congregation for almost ten years. In that time, the congregation watched Chad's two sons grow up. The older son, Carl, had since married, moved away, and now had children of his own. The younger son, Brad, still lives at home and is a rather flamboyantly effeminate man. When he was a teenager, his antics were written off as "being goofy," but everyone noticed that Brad never really dated or seemed interested in the opposite sex. No one ever directly accused Brad of being a homosexual, and no one in Brad's family ever said anything about it one way or the other.

The crisis came when Chad, who has taught the main auditorium class for eight years, suggested last Sunday that the church might need to reevaluate its stand on homosexuality. He did not directly advocate accepting homosexuality as an appropriate lifestyle, but called into question Christianity's contemporary and historical treatment of homosexuals. He also questioned whether or not a non-practicing homosexual should be allowed to be fully in fellowship with their congregation.

The class generated a hot, hostile debate. A couple of people stood up and walked out of the class in protest, and many others vowed not to return until Chad was ousted and they had a "biblically sound teacher." One person called for a meeting with the eldership. Only a handful of people were vocal in supporting Carl's statements, but they were mocked and ridiculed by the rest of the class. Anyone else who might have agreed with Carl was too ashamed or embarrassed to speak out. Regardless of where a person stood, virtually everyone in the class believed Carl was speaking out on homosexuality because of his son Brad. By the time worship was over that Sunday morning, the leadership of the downtown Central Church knew they were in for a tumultuous time. They felt torn by their own identity as both biblically sound and compassionate to outsiders, wondering if it was possible to be the same to insiders.

How did the above account of the fictitious downtown Central Church make you feel? What would you think or say? If you pursue this assessment process, it won't be long before you have to engage in some really difficult conversations; conversations whose outcome will radically affect the way your congregation views and encounters Christian marriage. The culture is never static. Both secular culture and church culture will continually present challenges to your theology and practices. As you build your marriage ministry, you must constantly think about how you will engage the difficult conversations, and being proactive, you will want to have considered these issues *before* they come up. In the following pages, I will discuss some of the more prominent difficult conversations you will want to consider. As always, the conversations I list are only a starting point. Many more will come out in your own unique context and in your marriage ministry team's discussions.

As we enter into these discussions, please understand that in asking the questions in each section below, it is not my intent to persuade you in any particular direction or to make a personal statement on the issues being discussed. I am simply raising questions that you already are or undoubtedly will be facing as you tackle the difficult conversations ahead. So please do not assume that I am for or against anything in particular or of a specific mindset about any given issue. The conversations being addressed are always shaped by the individual circumstances of the couple or couples involved as well as the context of the community of faith of which they are a part.

All or none

If you are coming into this process from a church that has a long history of "the church face" mentality (see chapter one), couples in your church might swing to one of two extremes. The first extreme is to avoid any real authenticity in favor of perpetuating the illusion of calm waters. If we don't talk about the bad things going on at home, then at church we can pretend like they don't really exist. So, how do you change decades of bad church culture? This is a tough hurdle to overcome and you need to proactively find ways to address it. Your leadership will play a pivotal role by how willing they are to be authentic about their own marriages.

The opposite extreme is a "too much information" culture. While a lack of transparency and openness can be problematic, you don't want to foster a community in which couples continually air their dirty laundry for the whole congregation to know. Regrettably, there are some individuals and couples who lack appropriate filters in sharing and discussing personal information. Promoting a culture of openness might give them permission to say or reveal anything, even information that could be detrimental to their marriage or would best be addressed in a confidential setting.

How can your marriage ministry team achieve a balance of fostering a culture of authenticity while still maintaining appropriate discretion? Every couple needs a group of friends within the church community with which they feel comfortable being honest and real. Sometimes, it might be a gender exclusive group. There are certain struggles in marriage that husbands need to share with other men and wives need to share with other women. There are also struggles couples need to share with other couples. Helping couples recognize and establish the appropriate balance early will circumvent many problems later on.

Test tube babies and beyond

Okay, nobody uses the term "test tube babies" anymore, but is the use of reproductive sciences always acceptable, or can it be harmful to marriage in some cases, or is it inherently detrimental to God's design for marriage? As much as everyone would like to relegate this discussion to being a private, personal decision between a husband and wife, there are both ethical and spiritual implications that really do affect the whole church culture.

This conversation goes well beyond whether or not it is right or wrong to facilitate a couple having a baby utilizing the couple's own reproductive systems. This is a discussion about where life begins and what extent a couple is willing to go to, to create life. Do we have the right to monkey around with the way God designed our bodies? Is there a divine reason a couple might not be able to conceive? What about frozen embryos that are left over after an embryo implants and the pregnancy takes? Is the use of a sperm donor tantamount to adultery? What does it communicate to your congregation about your beliefs of marriage when a single woman uses sperm donation to avoid the sin of premarital sexual intercourse and still has a baby outside the covenant relationship of marriage? What will your congregation's response be when genetics advances to the point of choosing a child's gender, eye color, intelligence, athletic ability, or other factors that will eliminate "the undesirable" elements of society?

Further complicating this discussion is the role children can play in a marriage, particularly if the desire for a child outweighs everything else for a couple. Children, by their very nature, are self-centered and demanding. In circumstances of normal conception, it is easy for a couple to allow a child to move into the center of the family, replacing the marriage as the foundational relationship of the family unit. Once there, the child will do everything he or she can do to maintain that position of prominence and power within the family structure. If a couple expends incredible efforts financially, physically, and emotionally to have a child through reproductive sciences, the child can quickly become all-consuming to the couple, even devouring their marriage and their faith, if they are not careful. The use of reproductive sciences can curse a couple as quickly as it can bless a couple if they are not able to maintain a godly perspective, especially if all their efforts still do not result in the conception of a child.

Having children will always be a personal choice and a personal journey for couples. But ultimately, the use of reproductive sciences does affect the culture of marriage in your congregation. And you clearly communicate something, either officially or unofficially, about the church's relationship to marriage by how you engage this conversation. Again, in asking the questions above, it is not my intent to persuade you in any particular direction or to make a personal statement on reproductive sciences. I have known couples who have gone through in-vitro fertilization who have a strong, godly marriage and are wonderful parents with well-adjusted children. I have also known couples who have gone through it and it has consumed their marriage. My objective is to lead you to consider the implications of this difficult conversation. Regardless of how you answer the questions above, and regardless of your feelings about the ethics and boundaries of any dimension of reproductive sciences, you must remember to continue to live in grace, mercy, forgiveness, and holiness, ministering to couples and individuals at your congregation.

How should the church engage the culture?

Throughout history, this has long been a debated issue. Do we withdraw from culture? Do we confront culture hostilely, as if it is the enemy? Do we seek to reform culture from within? From without? If your marriage ministry pursues a path of withdrawal, do you inadvertently set up the enticements of the culture as forbidden fruit? If your marriage ministry embraces the culture, do you give permission for reckless indulgence? One thing is certain, culture is never static, and your cultural context will always affect your congregation and the marriages within your congregation.

The fear in this conversation is in straddling the line between irreverence and irrelevance. How do you make Christian marriage relevant to your time and context without losing the divine purpose of Christian marriage for the kingdom of God?

Money, money, money

The two strongest indicators of a person's priorities are where they spend their time and their money. You can tell me anything you want to about what you believe and what you think is important, but show me your check book register and your daily schedule and I'll tell you what really is a priority to you. Finances are always a reflection of a couple, of their priorities, of their unity (or lack of unity), and most significantly of their faith. Historically, finances and financial difficulties are a leading cause of marital stress and marital failure.

With the substantial impact financial issues can have on marriage, what is your congregation doing to address this conversation? There are a number of good, Christian-based financial programs out there that you can offer to couples in your church. In addition to the physical and psychological side of this equation, are you also proactively addressing finances in marriage as a spiritual issue? Remember, if things are not right in a marriage relationship prior to having money, no amount of money in the world will fix it. Money is always a huge indicator of integrity, love, and respect for your spouse.

Mental illness and psychological changes

A few years ago I had a severe head injury. As a result of that injury, I was bed-ridden for nine days. Though I have less than an hour of collective memory from that nine days, my wife later shared some interesting accounts of what happened during that time. Although I do not remember much of anything, my wife clearly remembers how my head injury completely reoriented her world. The most significant change was a fundamental shift in my personality. To quote my wife, I became "very, very mean." She said I spoke harshly and critically when I spoke at all, yelling at her and snapping at our children. The reality of how different I was during those days sank in when Lisa later shared with me that she feared our oldest daughter Chloe would be the only one who would remember "how Daddy really was." As the days slowly ticked by and Lisa didn't see any notable changes in my condition, she started to brace herself for the reality that she was going to have to care for an ornery, inconsiderate, bed-ridden husband for the rest of her life. She was trapped with just memories of what life was and fantasies of what life should have been.

Through constant prayer and by the grace of God, I've had a nearly full recovery from the injury. (I haven't been able to smell or taste anything since, but all things considered, I'll take it.) "In sickness and in health, till death do we part" has a whole new meaning for me. Lisa was prepared to honor her vow and tend to a mentally incapacitated husband for the rest of her life. Thankfully, she didn't have to go through a long, drawn-out incident or have to figure out the logistics of coping with a spouse's prolonged illness.

There are few words that are more loaded, liberally used, and often abused than "crazy." Yet mental illness and severe psychological changes can rock a marriage to its core and potentially have an adverse affect on an entire congregation. Depression. Bi-polar disorder. Obsessive compulsive disorder. Kleptomania. Alzheimer's. Schizophrenia. Post-traumatic stress disorder. Post-partum depression. Creutzfeldt/Jakob (commonly called "mad cow") disease. Seasonal Affective Disorder. Anxiety disorders. Extreme phobias. Paranoia. The list of potential mental conditions that can affect a couple is incredibly lengthy.

Sometimes, we demeaningly label a person's personality and natural disposition as "crazy," particularly if it conflicts with our own disposition. Sometimes we call a person "crazy" because the way they express themselves is regionally or ethnically driven, and presents behaviors that, while acceptable in one place, are strangely foreign in another. And frequently, spouses in conflict can portray specific behaviors exhibited by the other as "crazy" in an attempt to assassinate their spouse's character or to gain or maintain some type of control in the relationship. While these types of situations need to be addressed, true mental diseases and illnesses are a totally different matter.

Hopefully, a couple was upfront with each other about any diagnosed mental conditions or known family history of mental illness before they ever said "I do." But how will your congregation help couples wrestle with the unexpected? The onset or worsening of mental conditions that affect a marriage can happen gradually as a disease progresses. Or, they can happen as quickly as a split-second car crash that causes permanent brain damage, as a result of a childhood violation that destroys someone's innocence, or from a violent crime that indelibly scars someone's psyche for life. A marriage-shaking mental change can last a short time or it can last a lifetime. Some conditions can be well-controlled by therapy and/or medication, and some may never be controlled or corrected.

Does your congregation have resources for helping couples? Are support groups available for various conditions, and if not available in-house, do you know where to refer someone? Is there a litmus test for confronting someone who's unjustly portrayed his or her spouse as "crazy"? How does the church family help couples honor their commitment to stand beside each other "in sickness and in health" when the sickness is beyond anything a husband or wife ever imagined?

Cross-cultural marriages

The stigma of so-called "mixed marriages" is becoming increasingly less significant in most places. However, there are still some areas of the country where marriages that cross ethnic boundaries are frowned upon, and perhaps even persecuted. If you do not already have any cross-cultural marriages, is your congregation prepared to show love and hospitality? If you are in a congregation that has a large population of cross-cultural marriages, are you helping those couples to navigate the issues inherent in such unions?

What about divorce?

Although this is not a book on divorce and remarriage, one of the most difficult conversations is, is there ever a time to accept divorce as inevitable, and possibly even preferred to the current circumstance in which a couple is living? What about separation? Can separation be beneficial for a couple? How will you integrate counseling into volatile marriage situations that are heading toward divorce? As I said at the outset, it is ultimately up to the couple whether the marriage succeeds or fails, but what is the church's role in addressing counseling, separation, or divorce? And, how might your positions and actions impact your overall marriage context?

What constitutes infidelity?

It used to be that the only definition for infidelity was sexual intercourse with someone other than your spouse. Everything else was "harmless flirting." So long as "nothing happened," there were no grounds for concern. But are their other types of infidelity other than physical infidelity? The concept of emotional infidelity is getting more and more attention. While emotional infidelity doesn't involve physical sexual contact, it does constitute taking the emotional energy and relationship investment that rightfully belongs only to your spouse and giving it to another. With the explosive growth of social media over the last few years, some individuals are living in a fantasy world with real people with whom they have connected or reconnected. Emotional infidelity might never lead to physical infidelity, but it is still a breaking of trust with your spouse, it is shrouded in secrecy and deception, and it is a huge stepping stone toward hardening your heart against your marriage covenant. Maybe that's why Jesus said looking at another lustfully is still committing adultery, even if you never touch the other person (Matt. 5:27-28).

It is tough to put an exact definition on infidelity, and the point a relationship becomes infidelity might be different from one couple or one person to another. Infidelity can happen physically, emotionally, socially, and even spiritually. Not all forms of infidelity carry the same level of consequences, but any infidelity creates a wedge in your marriage. It is critical that your marriage ministry team constantly discuss what infidelity is and what avenues the culture is creating for infidelity to slip into marriages within your congregation.

Abuse

Like infidelity, the definition of what constitutes abuse is much broader than just physical abuse. There are a number of ways husbands and wives can abuse each other. And the methods of abuse are varied and plentiful. Everything from words to finances to friendships to family connections can be used to belittle, intimidate, and attempt to control your spouse.

Your marriage ministry team will need to talk through ways to help a spouse who is being battered in an invisible way, as well as those who are being physically tormented. And remember, even though the stereotype is a thug husband beating on his helpless wife, abuse can very easily go both ways. Will you have a plan in place to identify abuse and help both spouses walk through this dark valley?

Pornography addiction

Pornography is an ever-present reality among couples. If you are not proactive about addressing the topic, providing accountability groups for both men and women, and giving your couples viable ways to protect themselves, then you will be reacting to the marriages that are torn apart because of porn. In chapter one, I covered pornography as an influence on marriage through the secular culture. Pornography reduces the sexual act to something selfish that objectifies the people involved. It obliterates the holy and God-ordained aspect of the sexual relationship and ruins true intimacy between a husband and wife. No one, male or female, is one hundred percent safe from pornography's influence, and anyone who claims to be needs to be careful lest he or she falls (1 Corinthians 10:12).

Make no mistake, pornography is a sin that will destroy marriages in your church and have eternal consequences on the souls of those involved. Like alcoholism, once it enters your life, you might seize and maintain control over the addiction, but it is an addiction, an always-present danger. You can never take for granted that you will not fall into the trap again, lest you let your guard down and give Satan an even stronger foothold. Because pornography is so addictive, so wide spread, and so easily concealed, your team needs to have serious conversations on how to help couples deal with it, both preventatively and in attending to addictions that are already present.

Women's role

As you move to view and facilitate marriage as a joint participation in the kingdom of God, your congregation's tradition and history of a woman's place in service may come into question. Part of the assessment process for your congregation might have to include a review and reflection on the opportunities and limitations of a woman's role in your church.

Hopefully, your goal in having this conversation will be to find avenues for couples to jointly participate in the kingdom, but still maintain the unity of the body of Christ and honor the theology of your fellowship. Your leaders will likely play a critical part in this discussion, as they will need to provide sound, contextually relevant, biblical reasoning for your congregation's practices in regard to women's role.

Blended families

Every type of family brings its own set of issues to the table. Just like cross-cultural marriages, blended families have situations that are entirely unique to their circumstances. For some congregations, blended families have been a part of the church culture for so long the church has already adapted, but for others becoming familiar with the needs of blended families will be a whole new experience. Because of the ever-rising number, conversations about blended families are absolutely critical for every church having an informed view of marriage.

Homosexuality

Almost everyone knows someone who claims to be homosexual, either a family member, a co-worker, a neighbor, or some other acquaintance. Accounts constantly surface of husbands or wives who, sometimes even after decades of marriage and raising a family, decide to "come out of the closet" and end their marriage covenant to be with a same-sex partner. And this is not just happening in the secular culture. It is happening in churches across America. If you do not believe that homosexuality is affecting the view of marriage in your congregation, please recognize that it will affect your children and your grandchildren's view of marriage (and I suspect if you don't believe it is affecting your church's view of marriage now, you are in denial). In spring 2011, Thom S. Rainer, the President and CEO at Lifeway Publishers in Nashville, Tennessee reported that six in ten millenials (people born between 1980 and 2000) did not see a problem with two people of the same gender getting married.

The scenario presented at the beginning of this chapter is not a real situation, but similar situations are playing out all throughout churches in America. This will undoubtedly be one of the most significant, impactful conversations churches will have in the coming decades. Cultural views of homosexuality will affect your congregation's view of marriage in one way or another. If you don't engage the culture now on this topic, you might find yourself swept away by it. And rote condemnation or acceptance of homosexuality is not the same as discussing it in a manner that is productive to marriages in your congregation, a manner that will allow your congregation to be salt and light to those in your community.

Background

Although this conversation is more attuned to individuals and individual couples, understanding the power of one's background to shape his or her experience of marriage is necessary for a vibrant, proactive marriage ministry.

An individual's background is shaped through the home environment and experience of marriage the person grew up with, but also the church culture's teaching (or lack thereof) on marriage. Even though he desires healthy communication with his wife, all he saw growing up was his parents yelling at each other. She wants to be intimate with her new husband, but her youth and teen classes at church presented sex in such a negative, restrictive light that she still feels guilt and shame every time he tries to touch his new bride. He saw his parents praying together in good times and bad, so he's determined to have just as powerful a prayer life with his wife. Her church had an annual blessing service for couples who'd been married in the previous year, so she felt comfortable turning to her community of faith when she and her husband hit a crisis in their own marriage.

With the baggage of our backgrounds that we all bring into marriage, we are faced with a choice. You will either repeat or rebel against what you grew up with, and both responses can be either positive or negative depending on what you are embracing or rejecting. How will your team deal with your own church's history of teaching on marriage? How will you help couples to embrace the positive and reject the negative things that will affect their relationship with their spouse and with God?

For every conversation above, there are a dozen more difficult conversations that will occur in your unique context. As you and your marriage ministry team engage these difficult conversations, you are not out there on your own. There is a multitude of books and resources written from every conceivable angle for most of the conversations you will encounter. You have the wisdom of your congregation's leadership. You have the width and breadth of your membership from which to draw.

For some of the difficult conversations that come your way, you will find workable solutions. For others, you may never come to a really good conclusion. And for some, God might just bring you answers from places you never expected or imagined. Your task is to engage the conversations. Don't be afraid to ask questions, to make observations, and to challenge tradition or conventional practice. But be sure you are always doing so through the lens of Scripture with a deep-seated love and respect for the covenant relationship of Christian marriage and for the people whose lives intersect your conversations. Love God, love your fellow person.

Marriage is not perfect. Because we are products of a fallen world and forced to live in a fallen world, our "Adam-and-Eveness" continually rears its ugly head. You can't anticipate every possible scenario, but if you have a solid foundation, a sound theology of marriage, and a church community that is willing to minister, love, forgive, and work toward reconciliation, then you will be a long way down the road in handling difficult conversations and difficult circumstances.

Conclusion—Eating the Elephant

We live in a microwave society. We want it fast and we want it easy. Instant results and instant gratification are the trademarks of today's American culture. A marriage ministry that will alter the marriage culture of your congregation and that will become a part of the DNA of your congregation, a view of marriage that will be part of your identity as a congregation of God's people, a culture of couples' joint kingdom participation—well, that's a crock pot recipe. A crock pot recipe requires more thought and more work on the front end, it cooks slowly, it requires patience, and it occasionally has to be stirred.

At the beginning of this book, I invited you into the wonderful world of marriage ministry. The problem is that the invitation is the elephant in the room. The assessment process outlined in the preceding chapters is a large, daunting task. It will require time, volunteers, and resources. Once the assessment is done, it will require more time, volunteers, and resources to enact the ministry. It will require time, volunteers, and resources to carry out ministry initiatives. It will require time, volunteers, and resources to keep the ministry going. It will require time, volunteers, and resources to stay abreast of all the dimensions of congregational life and the secular culture that will continually affect marriages at your church. If you embrace the assessment process in this book, everything it will lead you to is completely counter-cultural to our "I want it all and I want it now" American mentality. The invitation is offered, but there's a mighty big elephant in the room.

So what do you do? If Christian marriage matters, if you want your congregation to be something different than what it is now, if you're willing to make the sacrifices necessary to change your church for generations to come, if you want the culture of marriage at your church to be a witness to your community that presents marriage as something different than what the world offers, then you have to jump in with both feet. There's a big elephant in the room and it needs to be served up for dinner. But it's so big. How in the world can you eat an elephant? Everyone knows there's only one way to eat an elephant—one bite at a time.

When I was working on my doctorate, I had everything I needed to complete the task—approved thesis idea, a solid outline, a tight but workable timetable. All I lacked was the motivation to actually start. This was the biggest academic task I'd ever tackled. What if I failed? What if I wrote and wrote, but then what I wrote was rejected? I questioned every aspect of what was before me. It just loomed so large in front of me. Then, my friend John, who'd gone through the same program a few years earlier, gave me some great advice. "Just start writing." He went on to remind me that I'd wanted this degree for a long time. I'd done all the other class work to bring me to this point. Why let fear cause me to fail to accomplish what I knew needed to be done? I had to take the first bite. Write the first sentence. I'd love to tell you that after that it was easy, that everything just flowed to perfection. But it didn't. I had to go through multiple revisions. I struggled with what to say and how to say it. The things that had once been so crystal clear in my mind were being challenged both by my own ongoing research and the insights of others. Still, I kept plugging away. Sometimes I was discouraged. Sometimes I was jubilant. Regardless, I kept on writing. Eventually, I finished. I ate the elephant, but I had to take the first bite.

The easiest thing you can possibly do is nothing. Continue to be reactive when marriages collapse. Continue to bemoan the state of marriage at your church. Continue to pretend "those marriage problems don't happen here." Continue to put on your "church face" every Sunday and go talk to all your friends who are wearing their "church faces." But you know you can't do that. You know something needs to be done, or you wouldn't have picked up this book. Now do it. Accept the invitation. Eat the first bite. Then stand back and watch God work.

As your church engages in the assessment process outlined in this book,
go to The Marriage-Friendly Church blog site at
www.marriagefriendlychurch.blogspot.com
to ask questions, share your congregation's progress, and encourage other churches to help create an environment that will reclaim marriage for the Kingdom of God.

For weekly posts for couples that will enrich your marriage and challenge you to become more of what God is calling you to be, check out The Marriage Blog at www.rememberingourfirstlove.blogspot.com.

Communication—Handling Conflict—Intimacy—Commitment—Expectations—Recreation—In-laws and Extended Family—Love—Sex—Motivation—Finances—Background—Perspective—Humor—Covenant—Marriage and Culture—And More

To schedule Dr. Camp for a leadership training in proactive marriage ministry or couples' retreats, seminars and workshops for marriage enrichment, or other speaking, teaching, and preaching engagements, email him at dfcamp@gmail.com

CPSIA information can be obtained at www.ICGtesting.com
Printed in the USA
LVOW012355200213

320902LV00004B/8/P

9 780890 985359